The Little Guidebook for Smart and Resourceful Girls

THE GIRL'S BOOK OF ADVENTURE

Michèle Lecreux with Célia Gallais
and Clémence Roux de Luze

Illustrated by Jocelyn Millet

BARRON'S

CONTENTS

Cooking
❦ with HONEY ❦

WHAT IS HONEY?

Bees produce it. They feed on flowers and then store their harvest in the cells of their hives. Little by little the nectar turns to honey, which bees use as food. Honey is composed of nearly 80 percent sugar; it also contains water, minerals, and vitamins. Mixed with water, honey was used by the athletes in the ancient Olympics to recover their strength quickly. The benefits of honey have been known for thousands of years!

This natural wonder can give you beautiful skin, and it also has great cleanliness qualities. Honey helps in healing, falling asleep, and calming some stomach pains, plus it fights colds and sore throats.

❧ SWEET RECIPES ❧

These recipes will make you want to eat honey more often!

The Yogurt of a Thousand and One Nights

This is one of the oldest desserts and certainly one of the best!

Serve yourself some cottage cheese or Greek yogurt.

Add 2 teaspoons of good honey (organic if possible), a handful of dried fruits (apricots, raisins), and chopped dry roasted nuts (pistachios, almonds, hazelnuts).

Gypsum Roses

In the desert, gypsym roses are rocks that look like rose petals.

Just like these delicious little desserts!

INGREDIENTS
- 7 OUNCES (200 G) OF PASTRY CHOCOLATE
- 2 TABLESPOONS OF HONEY
- ¾ CUP (150 G) OF CORNFLAKES

SPECIAL ITEMS
- CUPCAKE PAPERS

1
Melt the chocolate squares in a nonstick pan over medium heat. Add the honey and mix well with a wooden spoon.

2
Put half of the cornflakes into a shallow dish and pour half the chocolate over them.

3
Stir gently. Add the rest of the cornflakes and continue stirring until they are well coated with chocolate. Pour on the rest of the chocolate and mix well. When the cornflakes are all thoroughly coated with chocolate, use a soupspoon to put small portions into the cupcake papers.

4

Now leave your gypsum roses in the refrigerator for about two hours. The chocolate will harden and you will have a delicious dessert that both young and old will enjoy.

❧ SWEET AND SALTY RECIPES ❧

Honey is not just for desserts!
A spoonful in dressing gives a hint of sweet.

 ## Bread with Honey and Goat Cheese

Bread with goat cheese is delicious and really quick to make. Enjoy it with a nice, crispy leaf of lettuce and tasty tomatoes sprinkled with a bit of olive oil.

INGREDIENTS

- 1 SLICE OF COUNTRY HEARTH BREAD
- 1 LOG OF GOAT CHEESE
- BUTTER
- HONEY

1

Ask an adult to heat the oven to 400°F (200°C). Butter the slice of good country bread. Put several slices of goat cheese on top.

2

Put your bread with the cheese into the oven for eight minutes. Remove it carefully and put a good spoonful of honey onto the cheese. Have the adult put it back into the oven for four minutes, and then enjoy!

Carrot and Honey Fries

You can serve this dish with rice or couscous.

1

Get help peeling and cutting up the carrots into sticks and preparing the bouillon with 1 cube and 10 ounces (.3 l) of boiling water.

INGREDIENTS

- 8 CARROTS
- 1 TABLESPOON OF HONEY
- 2 TABLESPOONS OF FRESH CREAM
- 1 BOUILLON CUBE
- 3½ OUNCES (100 G) OF THIN BACON
- SALT AND PEPPER

2

With adult help, brown the bacon in a deep frying pan. Add the carrots, the salt, and the pepper, and cover halfway with the bouillon. Add the honey and mix well. Simmer for twenty–thirty minutes, until the carrots are tender. Add the cream and cook five more minutes while stirring.

BON APPÉTIT !

MAKE A SWING!

There's no age limit for having fun on a swing! You can dream with your feet in the air and your hair in the wind.

A TIRE SWING

MATERIALS
- I OLD TIRE FROM A 4 X 4 OR A PICKUP TRUCK
- I STRONG, THICK ROPE ABOUT 10 FEET (3 M) LONG

1 Make sure there are no nails in the tire. Then take some time to wash it thoroughly in soap and water.

2 To keep water from collecting inside the tire when it rains, ask an adult to drill five or six small holes.

3 Find a tree with a branch strong enough to hold your weight and the weight of any other people who will use your swing. Ideally, the branch should be about 8 feet (2½ m) from the ground and be at least 6 feet (2 m) long, so you can hang your swing in the middle.

6 feet (2 m)

8 feet (2½ m)

4 👉

Ask an adult to tie the end of the rope to the branch using a bowline knot (see page 12). Use an overhand knot (see page 12) to tie the other end of the rope to the tire on the side opposite the little holes.

Test the strength of your swing before climbing on, then fly away!

A BOARD SWING

MATERIALS

- 1 THICK WOOD PLANK APPROXIMATELY 3 FEET (1 M) LONG AND 16 INCHES (40 CM) WIDE
- 2 THICK ROPES 8 FEET (2½ M) LONG
- SANDPAPER

1

Clean the plank, sand it smooth, and, if you wish, paint it your favorite color. Then varnish it to protect it from the weather.

2

Ask an adult to drill two holes in each end of the plank.

👆 *3*

Tie the ropes about 20 inches (50 cm) apart to a strong tree branch using a bowline knot (see page 12).

Pass each rope into one hole and then the other on the same end of the plank and tie an overhand knot (see page 12) above it.

☛ You can also decorate your swing with flowers or ivy to give it a nice touch, so it blends in more with the natural surroundings.

Use clear fishing line to hold everything in place.

Change the flowers regularly according to the seasons and your tastes!

Check to be sure that your swing is very strong before using it!

❧ Sailors' KNOTS ❧

Here are a few well-known knots you can use to tie your swing securely to a branch, or to tie up your boat to a mooring. Practice tying them until you get them perfect.

❧ BOWLINE ❧

This is a strong knot that is still easy to untie! To remember how to tie it, think of the phrase, "I come out of the well, go around the tree, and go back down into the well."

1 ☞ Here's the well.

2 ☞ Come out of the well.

3 ☞ Go around the tree.

4 ☞ Go back down the well.

5 ☞ Now all you have to do is pull tight!

❧ OVERHAND KNOT ❧

This knot is very useful for keeping something from slipping! It is easy to make, but not always easy to undo. It is also called the figure-eight knot.

1 ☞ Make a loop.

2 ☞ Go under the rope.

3 ☞ Then go into the loop from the top.

4 ☞ Pull tight!

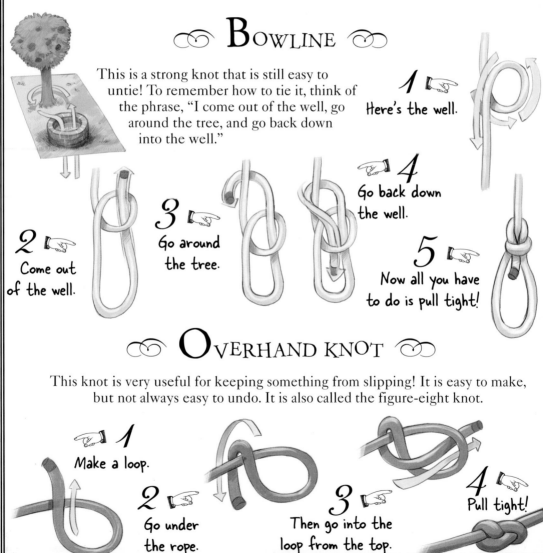

SQUARE KNOT

This is an easy knot to tie. It can be used for tying
two ropes together or for tying laces.

1 ☜

Make a first half hitch with
the ends of two different ropes.

☜ 2

Next, make
another knot but in
the other direction.

3 ☜

Tighten and check the
strength of the knot.

FISHERMAN'S BEND

The fisherman's bend is used for attaching a rope to a ring or other object
to keep it from sliding. Careful: Once it's tight, it is difficult to untie!

1
First make
three round
turns.

2
Pass the short
end through the
two loops formed
by the round turn.

3
Now make the
first half hitch
as shown.

4
Now make
a second
one in
the same
direction.

5
Pull tight
to keep
everything
together.

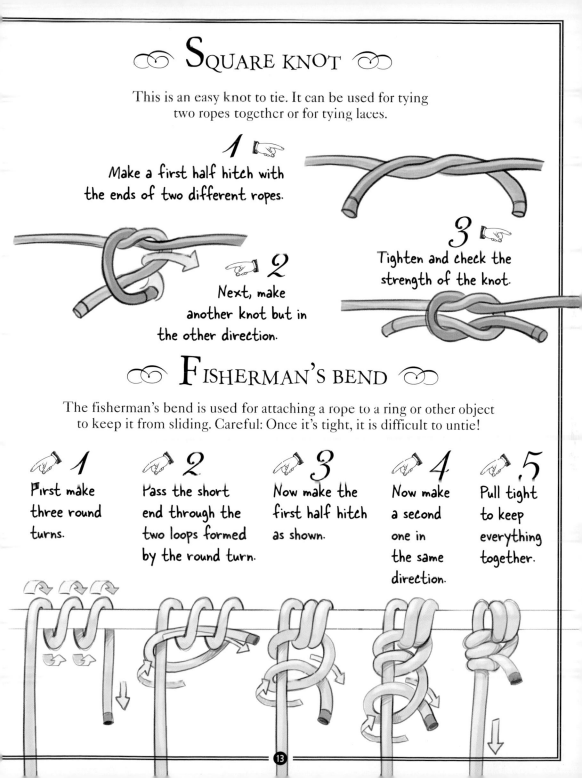

❧Beauty *Tips*❧

In both summer and winter, your skin needs protection and pampering so it doesn't dry out or peel, especially when you expose it to the wind, rain, and sun.

A BEAUTIFUL COMPLEXION IN A DISH!

To prepare your skin for the arrival of summer and to be ready with a beautiful tanned complexion, do a carrot cure: raw, grated, or cooked.

The beta-carotene will make you look great.

In addition, two vitamins that carrots contain help protect the skin and strengthen it against the wind and rain. These are vitamins E and C.

Vitamine E:
This is found in kiwis, avocados, almonds, and hazelnuts.

Vitamine C:
This is found in citrus fruits, strawberries, and peppers.

By eating all kinds of fruits and vegetables, you help your body and your skin!

☛ Do you know that, when you drink water, you also moisturize your skin? **Tip:** Don't hesitate to drink water regularly.

QUICK, A SCRUB!

A facial serves to clean your face. It removes all the dead skin and all the dust that's built up on your face. Mix a tablespoon of brown sugar with a half tablespoon of olive oil. Gently rub it into your face and neck with your fingertips and rinse carefully.

☛ Don't do a scrub too frequently; you might irritate your skin!

A HOMEMADE BEAUTY MASK

To make a quick moisturizing mask, crush a ripe avocado with a fork. Apply the resulting paste to your clean skin. Leave it on for five minutes and rinse it off with cold water. The oils contained in the avocado are very good for moisturizing your skin!

A NATURAL SCENT

Put the petals from four roses into a pan with 1 pint (1/2 l) of mineral water. With the help of an adult, put the pan onto a burner and heat the water. As soon as the water starts to simmer, remove the pan from the burner and let the petals sit for a half hour.

Strain the liquid. Pour it into a bottle or small jar that you can keep in the refrigerator for a whole week. You can use this rose water on your skin to refresh yourself and enjoy the scent.

WINTER'S COLD

☞ Here's a little tip for soft hands: Spread a thick layer of honey onto the back of your hands. Wait five minutes, then rinse thoroughly. Your hands won't feel the cold and the damage it causes!

Is your skin dry, tight, and a little red?

In the winter, your hands and face are the most exposed parts of your body.

Moisturize them every day with a really smooth cream, and don't forget your lips, or they will become chapped.

You can keep your skin from becoming rough by treating it this way every day. It will stay smooth, and this will also protect you against outside attacks of wind and cold.

Summer heat

At the beach in the summer, your skin dries out easily because of the sea salt. Use Tahitian monoï oil to moisturize your skin morning or evening.

This oil is made from tiara flowers in Polynesia. It is also used as a mask on damaged, dry hair.

⚠️ But be careful: This oil does not protect against the sun's rays, so it does not replace sunscreen, which is essential for guarding against sunburn.

By walking barefoot on the sand, your feet may become dry.

A solution! After taking a shower, dry your feet well and gently massage them with sweet almond oil. Pay particular attention to the heels, where the skin is thicker and drier.

✥ *Discover* Yoté ✥

This very ancient African game is a little like our game of checkers, but it has different rules.

Yoté allows you to take two of your opponent's pieces instead of just one if you succeed in jumping just one! Two pieces for capturing just one!

AN IDEAL GAME FOR THE BEACH!

You can play yoté at the beach by simply scratching out the board on the sand. You can also make your yoté board on a big piece of cardboard.

Draw a board with thirty squares: six lines with five squares each.

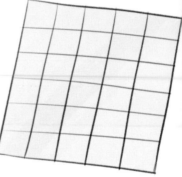

FIND THE GAME PIECES

Like checkers, yoté involves two players. Each player needs twelve game pieces.

Take a walk along the beach or next to a brook and pick up twenty-four shells, pebbles, little pinecones, bits of bark, or any other kind of plant.

To tell the game pieces apart, you can pick up two kinds of shells or pebbles, or make a mark on half of them with some paint.

THE RULES OF THE GAME: BETTER THAN CHECKERS!

In turn, the players can choose one of these actions: putting down a game piece, moving a piece, or capturing an opposing piece.

☞ Putting down a piece: onto any open square on the board!

☞ Moving a piece: always one square away, horizontally or vertically, as long as the new square is unoccupied. Note that diagonal movements are not allowed!

☞ Capturing an opposing piece: by jumping over it! The only way to capture an opposing piece is if it is on a square next to the piece to be moved, and the new square is open.

And still no diagonal jumps!

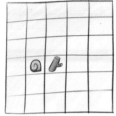 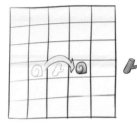

Another important rule: You don't have to wait for all your pieces to be on the board to move the ones that are already in play or to use them to make a capture!

☞ Here is the originality of yoté: As soon as one player succeeds in capturing an opposing piece by jumping over it, that piece is removed from the game once and for all, and that player has the right to remove another piece—any other opposing piece, no matter where it is on the board! You get to choose which piece is hurting your strategy for attack!

WINNING...

It's quite simple: The first player who takes all the opponent's pieces wins the game!

❦ PAPER Jewelry ❦

No need to spend lots of money to have beautiful jewels!
Just make them out of some pieces of paper!

MATERIALS
- SOME MAGAZINES
- SOME MATCHSTICKS
- A TUBE OF GLUE
- A PAIR OF SCISSORS

❦ PAPER BEADS ❦

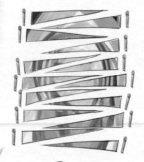

1 Choose a colorful page in a magazine and cut it out. Cut out some long triangles from this page; the base of the triangles must not be longer than a matchstick. The longer your triangle, the thicker the bead will be.

2 Roll up each paper triangle around a matchstick, starting at the base. Don't roll too tightly, because when you're done you will have to slide the matchstick out.

3 Before you finish rolling up the paper, put a small drop of glue onto the tip of the triangle. Hold this point in place for several seconds so it sticks.

4 Then slip the match out of the bead. Here's what you get: beautiful long, colorful beads!

☞ Tip:
To make beautiful, shiny beads, use aluminum foil!

A SINGLE BEAD

MATERIALS
- 1 THIN STRIP OF TWISTED FABRIC APPROXIMATELY 18 INCHES (45 CM) LONG
OR
- 1 THICK THREAD (OF THE SAME LENGTH)

A BASIC BRACELET

MATERIALS
- APPROXIMATELY 8 INCHES (20 CM) OF FISHING LINE

1 Make a single large bead. For this purpose, cut out paper triangles longer than the ones you made before.

2 Roll up several triangles, one over the other, remembering to glue the tip of each one.

3 String your bead onto the thread or the strip of cloth. Use a matching color. The result will be really chic! Now all you have to do is to clasp your necklace with a pretty knot that's easy to untie.

1 String your beads onto the fishing line and clasp it with a tight knot, and there you have it—a pretty bracelet you can wear or give as a gift.

A LONG NECKLACE

MATERIALS
- SEVERAL LENGTHS
OF FISHING LINE
APPROXIMATELY
3 FEET (1 M) LONG

If you have made lots of beads, make several long necklaces (like the "basic bracelet") and wear them together to look like a real star!

A COSTUME JEWELRY BARRETTE

MATERIALS
- 1 BARRETTE BASE
- SOME GLUE

1 Make about twenty paper beads of normal size. Very carefully put a little glue all along the barrette base. Make sure you don't get glue on your fingers!

2 Cover the barrette with beads arranged vertically and side by side.

Wait until everything is good and dry before using your new barrette!

🌿 A UNIQUE BROOCH 🌿

MATERIALS

- 3 THIN CORDS (OR STRING) OF DIFFERENT LENGTHS: 3 INCHES, 4 INCHES, AND 6 INCHES (7, 10, AND 15 CM)
- 1 SAFETY PIN

☞ **1** Make three large beads (see page 21, "A Single Bead"). Tie a knot at the end of each cord. String each bead onto a cord.

2 ☞

Attach them to the safety pin. Your brooch will look great on your blouses!

🌿 A VERY FASHIONABLE NECKLACE 🌿

MATERIALS

- 50 SMALL COLORED PLASTIC BEADS
- 1 LENGTH OF FISHING LINE ABOUT 2 FEET (0.6 M) LONG
- 1 LARGE NEEDLE

1 ☞ Make fifty paper beads of normal size. Using a needle, poke a hole in the middle of each of your beads as shown.

2 ☞ Slide the beads onto the fishing line, alternating the plastic beads and the ones that you have made, threading the line through the new holes. That way the beads are arranged in a nice pattern.

Clasp your necklace with a very tight knot. This necklace will give you a really stylish look!

Photos
⚘ *like the* PROS ⚘

Here are some ideas for
taking beautiful photos.
Grab your camera!

THE FIRST STEPS

Learn how to use your camera: What
adjustments do you have to make, how
do you delete a
photo, where is the
zoom, how do you
turn off the flash?

Whether or not
you are using your
camera, keep the
strap around your
wrist. That way
you won't drop the
camera.

Also remember to shut the camera off as
soon as you finish taking photos so you
don't waste the batteries, and, if there
is a lens cover, put it back into place.
If you now know how to use the camera,
here are a few simple tips: Set up
comfortably so you are not off-balance.
Take your time before pressing the
button! Try different framings, and

have fun! To avoid fuzzy pictures, hold
the camera as still as possible.

Give your camera time to make a couple
of corrections; push the button down
halfway. Then the corrections are
made automatically. Now push the
button all the way down to take your
photo. Click!

THE BASICS

🔊 Framing

Framing is the way you arrange the parts of pictures.

Professionals often use the rule of thirds. The idea is easy: Using imaginary straight lines, divide the scene into three equal parts, either horizontally or vertically.

In fact, some scenes work better in a rectangle that's taller than it is wide.

🔊 Light

The scene will look different very early in the morning or at the end of the day. The color shades will be different.

At the beach, for example, you can divide the scene into three horizontal parts: the sand at the bottom, the ocean in the middle, and the sky at the top.

Don't just take horizontal photos; remember to hold your camera vertically for some shots.

RESPECTING THE RIGHTS OF OTHERS

It is easy to take photos, but sometimes people in the pictures don't want others to see them. Always respect other people's wishes and photograph your friends only with their permission. Similarly, don't take pictures of strangers in ridiculous or dangerous situations. Always think about how you would feel in their place.

☞ People

To take beautiful photos of your friends and your family, you don't always have to put the subject in the center of the photo, or even use the flash indoors.

If there is enough light in the room, the natural lighting will give the faces softer, warmer shades.

To do a portrait of your uncle who is 6 feet 6 inches (2+ m) tall, get up to his level: If you need to, climb up on a chair! That way you will have a better portrait of him, a photo of his face down to the bottom of his neck or his shoulders.

On the other hand, for a good picture of your two-year-old cousin, crouch down and focus your camera on her face.

And pay attention to the background: You won't want to show a beautiful portrait if you see a trash can in the background!

MOTION

Many cameras have a sports function, which is shown by a picture of a person running. This function makes it possible to take several photos in a row, and break down the parts of a movement. Take your photo at just the right instant. This takes some practice!

Ask an athletic friend to jump into the air. After a couple of jumps, you will be able to take some neat photos!

ANIMALS

Photos of animals are not easy to take: Animals keep moving, or so it seems.

What's the secret of a great picture?

Be as invisible as possible and be patient—to the point that the animal you are photographing forgets you are there.

Don't forget to use your camera's sport function to capture the picture of your cat as it raises its head, a deer as it bounds away, or a seagull taking flight.

Also, consider what is important to you, what you want to see. And take advantage of the brilliant colors in nature.

Also respect your surroundings and don't trample all over the nature around you.

Show your PHOTOS

NATURE

Close-up photos of flowers are usually fairly easy to take.

There is a *macro* mode on many cameras. Get up very close to the chosen plant and move around it to find the best angle. Back up a tiny bit and wait to see if a butterfly or some insect lands on it.

There is nothing sadder than a photo forgotten in the memory card of a camera. After taking your photos, look at them and choose the best ones. Ask your parents to print them. You can use them as postcards, collect them in an album, display them in frames, and give them to your friends as gifts.

Play with the focus: The fuzzy part of a photo makes the clear part stand out. Your camera makes pictures that are sharpest in the center of the screen. Point at your subject, push the button halfway down, and then without moving your finger, shift your camera to change the framing. Your subject will be clear, but the rest will be blurry.

A beautiful picture is always a joy.

Do you have visions of a big pie? Neat! But watch out, little gourmet, keep a sharp eye peeled. Before you pick the little berries that grow on the bushes, make sure that they are **safe to eat!**

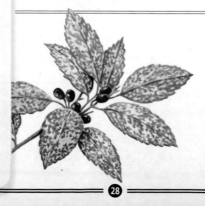

CAREFUL: POISON!

HERE ARE SOME BERRIES YOU MUST NEVER EAT. AT BEST, THEY WILL GIVE YOU A BAD STOMACHACHE; AT WORST, THEY CAN BE FATAL!

Wild but DELICIOUS!

CURRANTS

☞ Black, red, or white, currants grow on little low bushes in the summer. They are great for jelly, but what a job it is separating them from the clusters!

BLACKBERRIES

☞ Ouch! They grow on briars (bushes with thorns). Be very careful when you pick them! They are delicious when they are really black, in August or September.

☹ VIBURNUM

Similarities:
The leaves are a bit like those of currants.

The little red round balls look like currants.

Differences:
The flowers form large, white balls.

The fruits don't smell good. (You shouldn't want to taste them!)

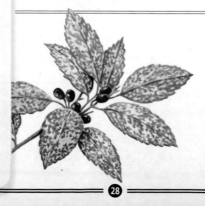

☹ ACUBA

Berries: They are shaped a bit like olives and are red.

Leaves: They are shiny and spotted with yellow.

RASPBERRIES
☞ These are the stars of the little red summer fruits because their flavor is great! They grow on bushes that may reach a height of 5 feet (1.5 m); each berry is on the end of a separate little stem.

☹ BITTERSWEET NIGHTSHADE

Similarity:
Little red fruits in clusters.

Differences:
The stalks may reach a height of 9 feet (3 m)

The purple flowers that accompany the berries,

☹ BRYONY

Similarity:
The little red berries in clusters.

Difference:
The whitish flowers that accompany the berries.

WILD STRAWBERRIES
☞ Well! Even though they are smaller than man-made strawberries, they are much sweeter! You pick them from small plants that grow low to the ground, and are accompanied by white blossoms with five petals.

Well-protected Fruits

Most little fruits are very fragile. If they get squashed, they turn into a nasty mush! And the stains they make do not come out! So carry them in a flat basket or in a little bucket. You can also make a custom holder!

1

Gently put the little red fruits that you have picked into a freezer bag, making sure to fill it only halfway.

2

Ask an adult to cut a plastic bottle in half.

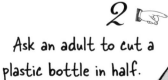

☞ **3**

Put the bottle over the half-full bag so that the top of the bag sticks out of the neck.

4 ☞

Then fold the top of the bag toward the outside and screw the cap back on.

Your fruits are now well protected thanks to the bag that hangs the length of the bottle!

Now you can carry them and enjoy them whole!

After gathering your fruits, you can make a dessert for the whole family!

❦ RED FRUIT ❦
Pie

PREPARATION: FIFTEEN MINUTES
COOKING: TWENTY-FIVE MINUTES
IN THE OVEN

INGREDIENTS
FOR SIX TO EIGHT PEOPLE

FOR THE CRUST:
- 6 OUNCES (175 G) OF BUTTER
- 1¼ CUPS (200 G) OF FLOUR
- 1 TEASPOON YEAST
- A LITTLE MORE THAN ½ CUP
  (100 G) OF SUGAR

FOR THE FILLING :
- APPROX. 2¼ CUPS (500 G)
  OF SMALL RED FRUITS
- 3½ TABLESPOONS (50 G)
  OF SUGAR
- 1 TEASPOON OF CORNSTARCH

UTENSILS
ONE PIE PAN

1 Melt the butter in a pan and remove it from the heat; add the flour, the yeast, and the sugar. Mix well.

2 When the dough separates from the pan, remove the pan from the heat.

3 Flatten out the dough on a flat work surface dusted with flour. You don't need a rolling pin; just flatten the dough with your (well-washed!) hands.

4 Spread the dough in the pie pan. Press firmly so that the dough fills the sides of the pan.

6 Pour the mix over the dough.

5 Mix the red fruits with the sugar and cornstarch in a bowl.

7 Ask an adult to bake the pie at 400°F (200°C) for twenty to twenty-five minutes. When the crust turns a nice color, the pie is done!

For Little GOURMETS

You can also bake mini-pies in individual molds. You can take these pies on a picnic to share with your friends.

The Hiker's *Toolbox*

So you have planned a hike with your family or friends. What a great idea! Here are some tips for dressing head to toe so you can guarantee a good day's fun.

SHOES

You can't put on just any old footwear! Even if you are a stylish dresser, forget about the flip-flops, the ballet slippers, and the dress shoes in your closet. You are going to be walking all day, and it is important not to have sore feet. Blisters can really ruin your outing. Choose a good pair of athletic shoes, or better yet, light, comfortable hiking shoes that support your ankles.

CLOTHING

Your clothing must be light, comfortable, and practical. Choose loose-fitting pants that don't make it hard for you to move. Natural materials such as cotton and linen are light and comfortable to wear.

☛ Tip:
If your shoes are new, wear them for a few days before your hike so that they soften up.

If you are going into the woods, don't wear shorts. Branches can scratch you, and nettles can sting! Also, depending on the weather forecast, dress in three layers: underwear, a T-shirt, and a sweater or a fleece for warmth. And a raincoat in case of rain!

The Essential
ACCESSORIES

☞ Don't forget your sunglasses, a tube of sunscreen, a cap or a hat, and a scarf for your neck: everything you need to protect yourself from the sun and possible sunburn.

☞ In case you get lost, it's a good idea to bring a compass, a map of the area, and binoculars.

Plus a flashlight in case you get surprised by nightfall!

☞ If you head out with friends, it's a good idea to spread out the items to carry so nobody's backpack is too heavy to carry.

☞ And if you are afraid of forgetting something, make a list a few days before!

REALLY NATURAL T-SHIRTS

If you head out for a hike to watch the animals, make sure you don't frighten them! It's a good idea to wear dark colors.

So forget your bright pink T-shirt or your colorful shirt, and take a simple white T-shirt that you have colored with plant dyes!

DARK COLORS FROM WALNUTS

When you gather walnuts, they are covered by a thick green hull, or outer covering that must be removed before eating them.

Get 1 pound (500 g) of these hulls and break them up into pieces. Put them into 5 quarts (5 l) of water and let them soak for a day.

Strain the liquid and put your white T-shirt in this bath for a day; it will come out with a very dark brown color.

OCHRE FROM ONIONS

Put a handful of onion peels in 5 quarts (5 l) of water.

With an adult's help, boil this mixture for twenty minutes. Remember to put a lid on your pan so that the water does not evaporate. Soak your T-shirt in the water until it takes on an ochre color.

CREAM COLOR FROM TEA

With an adult's help, pour boiling water onto the tea bag and leave it for at least a half hour. Then soak your T-shirt in this liquid. Put your pan back onto very low heat for a half hour.

You will really like the creamy blond color of your T-shirt.

PINK FROM BEETS

Cut a beet into large pieces.

Put these pieces into 5 quarts (5 l) of water to soak.

When the liquid becomes colored, strain it and soak your T-shirt in it until it turns a very soft pink.

Tip:
After dyeing your T-shirt, rinse it carefully
and dry it in the sun.

❧ CAMOUFLAGE DYES ❧

For a perfect camouflage T-shirt, tie
some knots in it to give it an irregular
shape.

Before putting your T-shirt in the dye
bath, tie one or more knots in it.

When you
untie your
T-shirt, you will
have designs similar
to flowers.

You can also use a string to
tie up a section of fabric.

The dye will not reach the
part of the cloth protected
by the knot or the string,
and it will remain white,
or at least lighter in color.

Flowers
on your PLATE

This little guide to flowers will allow you to add color to your dishes and to make your guests happy!

NONEDIBILE FLOWERS

Not all flowers can be eaten!

Be very careful: There are poisonous flowers that can easily be mistaken for edible flowers! This is why it's always important to know what you are doing before eating them, just as you would with mushrooms!

In addition, for recipes, do not use flowers that come from a florist because most of them contain pesticides, and they are very bad for your health. It's best to pick the flowers from your garden or in the wild.

PICKING FLOWERS

To gather beautiful, fresh flowers, it's

best to get up early, while the dew is still on the petals and the sun has not yet warmed up the plants.

Cut the flowers at their base, without the stem. Do the same if you want to gather the leaves.

CLEAN FLOWERS

To remove the little bugs that might be hiding inside and leftover pollen, carefully wash the flowers in clear water.

Put them onto a paper towel until they are completely dry, and then put them into a box or a tightly sealed plastic bag.

Flowers stay fresh for a good week when they are kept cool.

Certain flowers have a very noticeable taste (spicy, bitter, sweet). It's a good idea to sample them before putting a small quantity of them onto your plate!

Some recipe ideas!

 *Violet Syrup*

⚠ Get help from an adult for this recipe.

INGREDIENTS
- 5 OUNCES (150 G) OF VIOLETS
- 5 QUARTS (5 L) OF WATER
- 3¼ CUPS (750 G) OF SUGAR
- JUICE FROM ONE LEMON

UTENSILS
- 1 BOWL
- 1 WOODEN SPOON
- 1 EMPTY GLASS BOTTLE
- 1 PAN

Put the violet petals, without the green parts, into the bowl. Pour a cup (.25 l) of boiling water over them. Add the lemon juice. Cover and let stand for two hours. Pour the sugar and a cup (.25 l) of water into a pan. When the sugar is melted, bring the mixture to a boil and cook it for a while longer. Pour your violet water into the syrup. Mix with the wooden spoon, then let it cool before putting it into the bottle. You can enjoy your syrup with some added water or pour a few drops onto ice cream. The taste is surprising and the color is amazing! Your syrup will last for several days if it is kept cool and away from the light.

 Crystalized Rose Petals

Gently beat one egg white with a fork.

Using tongs, soak the petals one by one in the egg white. Coat the petals with sugar before placing them onto a platter covered with baking paper to keep them from sticking. The petals must not touch one another.

Let them sit in the open air for about twelve hours. They will dry and you can eat them just as they are or use them for decorating a cake.

INGREDIENTS
- THE PETALS FROM ONE ROSE, WASHED AND WRUNG OUT (Don't forget: Use an untreated flower from the garden and not from a florist!)
- 1 EGG
- A LITTLE MORE THAN ½ CUP (100 G) OF GRANULATED SUGAR

UTENSILS
- 1 FORK
- 1 BOWL
- WOODEN TONGS
- BAKING PAPER

FLOWER	USE	EDIBLE PART
✿ Begonia	• In fruit salad • Confit [1] • As a garnish	The flower.
✿ Nasturtium	• In salads • In butter • Confit	The flowers and the leaves. *The taste is peppery.* *A good seasoning for salads.*
✿ Edible Chrysanthemum	• In salads • In soups • In sauces	The flowers and the leaves. *The taste is bitter. The leaves are edible but the petals must be boiled in water for a few minutes before eating.*
✿ Poppy	• In syrups (cakes, ice cream...) • For decoration	Only the petals are used.
✿ Lilac Fuchsia	• Confit • For decoration	Only the petals are used.
✿ Daisy	• In salads • Confit • In mashed potatoes • In soups	The flowers. *The taste is a bit spicy.*
✿ Scented-leaf Geranium	• In salads • Confit • In herbal tea • For decoration	The leaves. *The flavor is similar to lemon mint.*

[1] *Confit : Something cooked slowly over very low heat with a little sugar or honey.*

FLOWER	USE	EDIBLE PART
✿ Pansy	• In fruit salad • Confit • In butter	The petals. *It's a good idea to remove the bitter stalk before use. The taste is sweet.*
✿ Dandelion	• In salads • Confit	The leaves. *The taste is bitter.* *The flavor is peppery.* *A good seasoning for salads.*
✿ Marigold	• In salads • In soups • In butter • In sauces • In biscuits	The petals and the leaves. *Marigold colors foods.*
✿ Sunflower	• In salads • In soups	The petals, the buds, and the roasted seeds. *The roasted seeds are edible and can be used anywhere: on cheese-topped dishes, in bread, cakes, and so on.*
✿ Tulip	• In salads • Confit • Stuffed	The petals. *The tulip has a slightly sweet taste.*
✿ Violet	• In salads • In vinaigrette • In syrups • In jelly	The flowers and the leaves. *It has a sugary taste.*

❧ *Precious* **Photos** ❧

How should you make your photos stand out?
Either by displaying them or by carefully keeping them
in a photo album. The choice is yours!

❧ A QUICK PICTURE FRAME ❧

MATERIALS
- 1 OLD CD
- 1 CD CASE
- PAPER OF DIFFERENT COLORS
- A PEN
- A GLASS
- A PAIR OF SCISSORS
- LIQUID GLUE

1
Choose a photo of a person or an animal
with the face centered in the picture.

2
Using the glass
and the pen, trace
a circle around
the face.

3
Cut out the
photo around
the circle and glue
it to the center
of the CD.

4
Cut out little designs,
such as hearts, from
different colored paper
and then glue them all
around your photo.

 5

Cut out a piece of colored paper in the shape of the CD case. Slide the CD and the square of paper into the case.

6 ☞

Open the case and put it onto your desk!

YOU CAN ADMIRE THE FINISHED PRODUCT!

A PERSONALIZED PHOTO ALBUM

1 ☞

Choose a nice close-up photo of your face in profile. Cut it out, following the outlines of the face and the hair.

MATERIALS
- A PHOTO OF A PERSON'S PROFILE
- 1 COLORED SHEET OF CARD STOCK (DIMENSIONS: TWICE THE SIZE OF YOUR PHOTO)
- SOME SHEETS OF PAPER
- A PENCIL
- A PAIR OF SCISSORS
- SOME STRONG THREAD
- A NEEDLE
- A RULER
- LIQUID GLUE

☞ **2**

Put the ruler behind the neck, straight up and down, draw a pencil line, and then cut along the line.

☞ **3**
Fold the card stock in half the long way.

☞ **4**
Glue your photo along the fold.

5 ☞
This cardboard will be the cover of your album. Close it and cut around the photo. That way your album will have a unique shape!

The pages of your album

☞ **1** Open up your album and lay it flat on one of the pieces of paper. Trace around the outline and cut it out.

2 ☞
Duplicate this shape on as many sheets of paper as you wish and cut them out. Place all the cutouts on top of one another, and using a needle (with the help of an adult if necessary), poke three holes in the centerfold.

4 inches (10 cm)

☞ **3**
Thread the needle. Push it through the middle hole and leave at least 4 inches (10 cm) of thread sticking out.

☞ **4**
Push the needle up through one of the other holes.

5
Then push it down
through the third hole.

6
Turn over all the pages and push the
needle back through the middle hole.

7
Turn the pages over again
and make a knot with the 4 inches
(10 cm) of thread previously kept in
reserve. Cut off any extra thread.

8
Glue the inside of your cover
all along the central fold.

9
Gently place the folded
pages on top the
outer fold of all
the pages on top
of the glued inner
fold of the cover.

Hold it in place for a few minutes
to let everything dry.

NOW YOUR ALBUM IS READY FOR
YOUR MOST BEAUTIFUL PHOTOS!

A Birthday Piñata

Traditionally in Mexico, during village celebrations, people filled a large clay pot, the piñata, with sweets and little toys. It was hung from a tree branch. In order to eat the treats, the children had to break the piñata by striking it with a stick, with their eyes blindfolded!

To liven up your birthday, you too can have fun with a piñata—without having to destroy a pot! Here's an easy way to make one.

MAKING A PIÑATA

MATERIALS
- 1 BALLOON
- A LONG, STRONG STRING
- FLOUR
- NEWSPAPERS
- A NEEDLE
- A PAIR OF SCISSORS
- PAINT
- A HOLE PUNCHER
- CONFETTI, CANDIES, LITTLE GIFTS…
- A PAINTBRUSH

1 Mix up a glue from equal amounts of flour and water. This glue is not very strong, but since the piñata is made to be broken, it will be perfect!

2 Blow up a balloon.

3 Cut out long strips of newspaper. Smear on lots of glue.

4

Put the strips onto the balloon and overlap them a little. Leave an open spot about 2 inches (5 cm) all around the knot in the balloon.

5

Let dry. When the paper piñata has dried, it is strong enough to keep its shape without the aid of the balloon. Use the needle to pop the balloon.

6

Paint your piñata. Put the candy and gifts in through the hole.

7

Using the hole puncher, make a hole on each side of the opening in the piñata.

8

Thread the string through these holes, and then hang up the piñata from a tree branch.

❧ THE PIÑATA GAME ❧

All your guests in turn have their eyes blindfolded. They try to strike the piñata with a stick and break it. Anyone can call out directions to the player. When the piñata gets hit, it breaks and everything inside falls to the ground in a shower of confetti!

MATERIALS
- 1 STICK
- 1 STRIP OF THICK CLOTH

Herbal *and* Wellness Teas

Do you feel like having a hot drink during a break? Prepare a 100 percent-natural drink that will be good for you. But don't drink more than three cups a day!

PICK CAREFULLY!

Of course, you can gather the plants and flowers for making the herbal and wellness teas suggested here. But be very careful, because many flowers look like other ones! Some of them may be poisonous! Just as you would do with mushrooms, show the plants you have gathered to an expert to get confirmation of their name and use.

CAUTION!

Don't take any needless risks! Whether you use a kettle or a pot to heat your water, be careful to avoid splashing or burning yourself! Always get help from an adult.

CAMOMILLE TEA

This flower is gathered in early summer. The chamomile flower looks like a daisy with a stem 4–12 inches (10–30 cm) long and a yellow, cone-shaped center.

To make chamomile tea, you need a tablespoon of dried flowers. Pour hot water over the flowers and let them sit for a good five minutes. Add a little sugar or honey. This herbal tea will help you relax and fall asleep.

THYME TEA

It is reported that during ancient times thyme was used to treat the battle wounds of warriors, and as a medicine for all kinds of problems. Do you have a cold or a sore throat? Then take a teaspoon of dried thyme. Let it sit for five minutes in hot water. Strain the liquid. Add a little lemon juice and a spoon of honey; this will make your throat feel better.

A MIX OF SPICES AND VANILLA

With an adult's help, put two sticks of cinnamon, four anise stars, three cloves, and a vanilla pod into a pint (½ l) of boiling water. After 10 minutes, carefully remove the spices. Add a little brown sugar to your mix.

This mix is particularly good for relieving stomach pains and aiding digestion.

SAGE TEA

Sage leaves were used as medicines to aid digestion and to calm people who felt ill at ease. In small quantities, they can be used to make a very tasty herbal tea.

All you have to do is pour some boiling water over a handful of fresh or dried sage leaves.

Remove the leaves as soon as the water takes on a pretty blond color.

Add a teaspoon of honey and enjoy!

MINT TEA

This is the traditional drink in the Maghreb (or northwestern Africa), and it's perfect for an instant change of scenery.

Boil a pint (½ l) of water and let it cool to room temperature. Now you need three large spoonfuls of green tea, some green mint, and five tablespoons of brown sugar.

Wash, cut up, and drain the mint. Put it on the bottom of the teapot.

Add the green tea and the sugar and let it sit for five minutes.

BON VOYAGE, AND ENJOY YOUR BREAK!

PREDICTING *the* Weather

Do you know that you can read the clouds?
Here are some hints that will help you predict the weather.

WIND DIRECTION

In most places, the wind that comes from the west brings rain. It has in fact passed over large bodies of water and is loaded with moisture. Eventually, the water vapor contained in the clouds condenses; that's why it rains. So when the wind comes from the west, you may need your umbrella or raincoat!

The wind that comes from the north has passed over the North Pole and is loaded with cold air. If it's windy out, quickly put on a warm sweater.

The wind that comes from the south has gone over warm regions. It brings dry, very warm air.

CLOUDS

There are several types of clouds. Learn to recognize them, for they will help you predict the weather.

☞ Cirrus

With their delicate form that makes them look like strands, they float very high in the sky. Because they are made up of ice crystals, you can predict that the weather will change when they arrive.

☞ Stratus

Gray, flying low, and forming a thick layer, these leave no doubt about the weather: Get ready for a day of fog and rain showers.

☞ Cumulus

These look like big bundles of cotton or a huge mound of cotton candy. Isolated in a blue sky, they bring fair weather; you have no cause for concern.

But sometimes they cluster together and form a dark mass that blocks the horizon. Then they are called cumulonimbus. In that case, get your rubber boots and your rain gear ready: There's a storm coming!

RAIN

Of course, if you are on vacation you want nice weather. And nobody really likes rain. But imagine a landscape where it never rained—a desert where nothing grows!

THE SUN

The sun's light and heat are a powerful source of energy, which is captured by the solar panels on the roofs of houses and turned into electricity.

WEATHER SURPRISES IN THE MOUNTAINS

If you are headed out for a hike in the mountains, don't put too much trust in the blue sky in the morning! In the mountains, the temperature can change very quickly: Always bring along a sweater and rain gear!

CHECK YOUR BAROMETER

If you have a barometer at home, check it! A barometer measures the atmospheric pressure from the weight of air masses. The high pressure that you sometimes hear mentioned in weather reports is a sign of good weather.

The air in a high-pressure system is "heavier" than that in a low-pressure system, which brings bad weather.

Look at what the needle shows: Is it pointing toward *good* or *bad* weather? Now you can have fun predicting the future.

A NATURAL BAROMETER

Do you know that there is a *natural* barometer? The simplest barometer is a pinecone.

Find a nice, big pinecone. Put it on the windowsill and look at it every morning. If it is all curled up, it is going to rain; but if it is open like a flower, the day will be nice and sunny!

No, there is no magic involved. It's just that the scales of the pinecone protect the seeds that the tree produces. To give the seeds the best chance of developing, they have to fall to the ground when the weather is right. That's why the pinecone opens to release the seeds only when the sun is shining and it is not raining!

And if you want your natural barometer to be pretty, you can disguise your pinecone to look like a person.

1 Glue a little Styrofoam ball from a hobby shop to the top of the pinecone to make a head.

2 Draw some eyes and a mouth on it.

3 Stick some pieces of cardboard into the sides to make hands.

4 If you wish, add an accessory: a little broom made from a twig, a little umbrella used to decorate cups of ice cream, or even a little flower.

HOW ABOUT THE ANIMALS?

Before we do, they sense the changes in the weather. So, if you like, try to observe the animals around you.

☞ **It will be nice weather if** the frogs croak at night, the crickets are chirping, you see lots of bats flying, or the ladybugs are happily feeding on the flowers.

☞ **It will be bad weather if** the spiders go back indoors to spin their webs in the house, the swallows fly low in the sky, the snails and slugs, which like the rain, are out and about, the bees remain in their hives, or your dog or cat seems a bit nervous.

So...

What will the weather be like tomorrow?

Discover **Furoshiki**

The Japanese know the
art of folding scarves!
Bags, clothing—here are the basics of furoshiki.

✤ AN ADORABLE TOTE ✤

To carry your snack, take a large square scarf
and fold it as follows:

1 Put your scarf down flat. Put what you want to carry in the center.

2 Tie the opposite corners of the fabric together.

3 Thread one of the knots under the other.

Handle

4 Pull a little to tighten and strengthen the bundle. The loop serves as a handle for your furoshiki cloth tote!

❧ A REALLY PRETTY HANDBAG ❦

This traditional folded project allows you to take personal items along as if you had a real handbag.

☞ **1** Divide what you want to carry into two piles. Put each pile on opposite corners of the scarf.

☞ **2** Fold the two corners toward the middle of the scarf, over each item.

☞ **3** According to the size of the scarf and the size of the items, fold the cloth with the items once or twice more toward the inside, until the two folds touch.

✍ **4** Now take the two corners that you haven't yet used, one in each hand. Fold the top one down, and the bottom one up.

5 ☞ Careful: This is the important part of this fold: Tie these two corners on the bottom. To tie this knot, turn the whole thing over. Bingo!

6 ☞ You have just made a very pretty bag!

🌿 A PRATICAL BACKPACK 🌿

When you are out and about, here's how
to make a quick little backpack so you
can bring back some pinecones and more
when you're on a hike in the woods. You will
need two scarves.

👉 **1** Place what you want
to carry in the center
of the first scarf.

👉 **2**
Tie two corners
together.

3 👉
Roll up the
second scarf
and then slide
it under the
knot you have just tied.

4 👉
Tie each end of this second scarf to the
free corners. This forms the two straps for
your backpack! Now all you have to do is
slide your arms through. Neat, huh?

🌿 A LITTLE VEST 🌿

To protect yourself from the sun during the afternoon, or from the cool breeze in the evening furoshiki is up to the task!

1 Fold a large scarf and tie the corners together two by two.

2 Turn the scarf inside out to hide the knots.

3 Put your arms through the opening at the bottom and stick one arm out of each side. There you go—very stylish!

🌿 BARE BACK 🌿

For this item, you need a large, square scarf and the help of a friend in tying the knots.

1 Hold the scarf by the two top corners.

2 Tie them behind your neck.

3 The two other corners are tied behind your lower back. Here's the back.

4 And the front! Pretty good, huh?

❧ Candles all YEAR LONG ❧

What's more magical than a light shining outdoors in the yard, regardless of the season?

☞ CAREFUL!

Before lighting a fire—even a tiny candle—ask permission from an adult and keep a bucket of water near the flame to put out any fire that gets away from you.

IN THE FALL: THE MINI-MONSTERS OF HALLOWEEN

Halloween custom involves carving pumpkins into jack-o-lanterns. Use some oranges instead!

MATERIALS
- SOME ORANGES
- AN EQUAL NUMBER OF TEA LIGHTS
- A FELT-TIP PEN
- 1 SMALL SPOON
- A KNIFE

1 ☞ Ask an adult to cut off the top quarter of the oranges.

2 Using a little spoon, empty out each fruit, being careful to avoid poking through the skin. Use the felt-tip pen to draw an ugly face on the orange skin. Be careful you don't cut yourself when you cut out the mouth, nose, and eyes of your monster with the point of a knife.

Houuuu...

3 ☞ Put a candle inside each fruit and light it. Now the mini-monsters can invade your yard!

🌱 IN THE WINTER:
THE CHRISTMAS CANDLE 🎄

Here's a very easy way to make natural mini-candles
to put side by side and make a dream yard.

MATERIALS
- A FEW MANDARIN ORANGES
- AN EQUAL NUMBER OF SAUCERS (OR JAR LIDS)
- SOME OIL
- A KNIFE

1 ☞ Cut off the top of the
mandarin oranges. With an adult's
help, use the point of a knife to
make a very smooth edge, or else use
your fingers to make a jagged edge.

☞ **2** Carefully remove the sections of fruits
without breaking the white stem in the center.
It will serve as a wick. Make sure you don't tear
the half of the skin that you want to keep.

3 ☞
Eat the sections of
mandarin orange!
Now, this is not
too useful in making
candles, but it
would be a shame
not to eat such
nice fruit!

4 ☞
Put each mandarin orange
skin onto a saucer. Pour a
tablespoon of oil into each
half-mandarin. Then pour
a little oil along the wick
so it soaks in well.

5 ☞
Ask an adult to light the top of the wick with
a match. There you have them—your mandarin
candles are ready to enchant the night!

In the springtime: ❧ Easter lamps ❧

Materials
- Some plastic yogurt containers
- An equal number of tea lights
- Tubes of paint

1 Carefully wash the yogurt containers.

 2

If you want to create colored light, first coat the whole container with a coat of paint mixed with lots of water.

3 ☞

Let it dry, then decorate each container with undiluted paint.

Careful! Choose a small, simple design, because the more room it takes up on the container, the more it will hide the light from the candle. Put the candles into the decorated yogurt containers.

❧ IN THE SUMMER: A BEACH LANTERN ❧

1 ☞ Ask an adult to pound down the edges of the can so you don't get cut. Also ask the adult to poke some holes all around the can using the hammer and the big nail. These holes can be arranged randomly or they can make a design (sun, hearts, stars).

☞ *2* Finally, you will need two large holes near the upper edge, on each side.

☞ *3* Thread each end of the string through the holes and tie a knot so you have a sort of handle. Coat the can with glue and roll it in the sand to decorate it. You can also glue on shells or little pieces of wood.

☞ *4*

Put the stick through the handle. This will allow you to hold the lantern away from you so you don't burn yourself. Put the candle into the can and ask an adult to light it. After nightfall, your lantern will light your little walks in the moonlight.

My **Organic** *Calendar*

Follow our fruits and vegetables calendar
to make recipes that are full of taste,
healthy, and respect nature!

SOUTH AFRICA

NO MORE SEASONS?

In supermarkets, we can find fruits
and vegetables throughout the year.
The green bean season runs from June to
September. During the other months of
the year, the store gets its supplies from
other countries.

This makes us think that these
vegetables grow 365 days of the year!
But that's not the case: There is a season
for every fruit and every vegetable.

WHY ORGANIC?

Growing organic means not using products
that are harmful to the earth and maybe
even to our bodies. Eating organic often
means choosing to buy products from the
area where we live, so delivering them
causes less pollution than if they came
from much farther away.

AT THE MARKET

It's best to know what fruits and
vegetables are currently in season and to
go to the market where the farmers sell
the products they grow themselves.

It is a real pleasure to see the colors
and smell the aromas of the fruits and
vegetables.

In addition, you respect the cycle of
nature when you eat seasonal fruits and
vegetables. This is the time when these
fruits and vegetables are at their best:
fully ripened, with lots of vitamins!

THE ORGANIC CALENDAR GAME

Give each member of your family a blank sheet of paper.

🐛 Have him or her draw four columns and write or draw the fruits and vegetables for each season within a time limit (one minute is fun!).

🐛 Take a big piece of cardboard. Make four columns, one for each season.

🐛 Then make as many lines as there are people in your family, plus one more for the "fruits and vegetables." Use this line to jot down the right answers.

🐛 Write the number of correct answers from each person on the other lines.

Who knows the most about fresh fruits and vegetables? Whoever has the most points, of course!

Cut off the top of your organic calendar. You can hang it up in the kitchen—a very useful little reminder!

	Spring	Summer	Fall	Winter
Fruits and Vegetables				
Dad				
Mom				
Nathan				
Nancy				

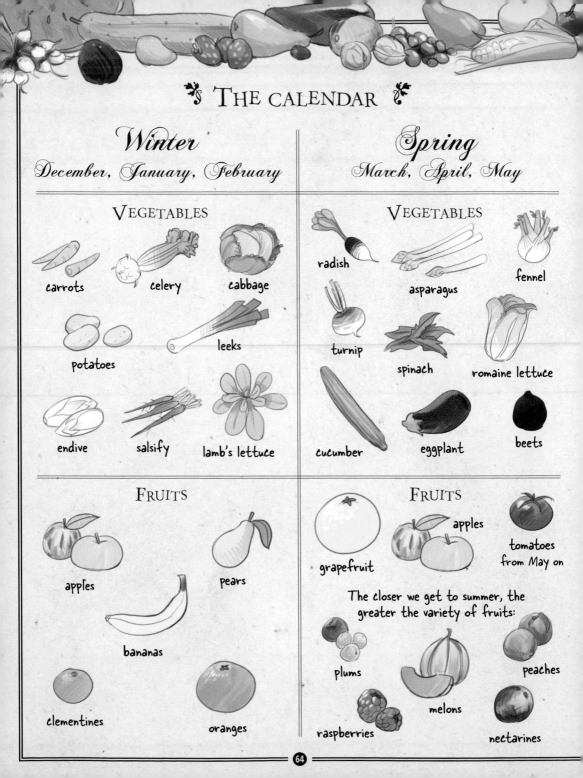

THE CALENDAR

Winter
December, January, February

VEGETABLES

carrots

celery

cabbage

potatoes

leeks

endive

salsify

lamb's lettuce

FRUITS

apples

pears

bananas

clementines

oranges

Spring
March, April, May

VEGETABLES

radish

asparagus

fennel

turnip

spinach

romaine lettuce

cucumber

eggplant

beets

FRUITS

grapefruit

apples

tomatoes from May on

The closer we get to summer, the greater the variety of fruits:

plums

melons

peaches

raspberries

nectarines

Summer
June, July, August

VEGETABLES

broccoli
from June
to October

artichokes
from June to
September

green beans
from June to
September

eggplant

bell pepper

cucumber

onion

peas
June/July

FRUITS

strawberries

cherries

blackberries

currants

blueberries

black currants

plums

peaches

nectarines

apricots

Fall
September, October, November

VEGETABLES

carrots

broccoli

cabbage

spinach

leeks

pumpkin

winter squash

Jerusalem
artichoke

FRUITS (AND SOME NUTS)

grapes

figs

apples

walnuts

hazelnuts

Japanese-style *Breakfast*

For a unique taste, turn to Japanese bento,
a really fun little box.

WHAT DO YOU PUT INTO IT?

The Japanese carry their lunches in boxes called *bentos*. Traditionally, a *bento* box is divided into several compartments in which there are rice, meat or fish, vegetables, and fruits. This is a very balanced meal. The box also includes sauce and little wood or plastic skewers for picking up the food.

The *bento* is even more fun for the kids! Generally, Japanese mothers take the time to make up fun and appetizing creations.

A BEAUTIFUL SAMPLING

Have fun decorating your food so it looks like cartoon characters. In Japanese, this is called *kyaraben*.

Use food coloring to color the rice, and carve the shapes of noses, eyes, ears, etc. in vegetables and fruits.

Create a scene with the characters made from the rest of the foods before eating them all up! Let your imagination run wild!

NATURAL COLORINGS

To color your rice, add a small spoonful of powdered saffron to the water to make it turn yellow, or tomato juice to make it red, or a slice of raw beet for pink.

Based on the color produced, you can make a pig, a baby chick, or a mushroom. Corn kernels can be used for eyes, a cherry tomato for a nose, a sliced radish for a flower.

ACCESSORIES

To carry your meal, use a pretty plastic box that you decorate with permanent markers. To make attractive shapes in a slice of ham or a thin slice of radish or carrot, there are cutters in original shapes in stores.

To make neat shapes in sandwich bread or cheese, for example, you can use a cookie cutter. And you can use a fine new artist's brush dipped in food coloring to draw on the food. Let your imagination run free!

❧ CUTE CREATURES YOU CAN EAT ❦

A Baby Chick

MATERIALS
- SOME RICE
- 1 OLIVE
- ½ CARROT
- 1 TEASPOON TOMATO SAUCE
- A PAIR OF SCISSORS

Color the rice yellow (see last page). Pack it into a soupspoon and make it oval in shape. With the pair of scissors, cut out small pieces of olive and carrot. The olive becomes the eyes, and the carrot is used for the comb, the beak, and the feet. Add a tiny bit of tomato sauce to color the cheeks.

That's all there is to it!

A Mouse

Hard-boil an egg. Also cook a green string bean. Use the latter for a tail. Raisins are the ears, and pieces of chive form the whiskers. For the eyes, you can either stick in two cloves or two pieces of olive. Cut off a piece from the bottom of the egg so it doesn't roll around in the box.

MATERIALS
- 1 EGG
- 1 GREEN STRING BEAN
- 2 RAISINS
- 1 PIECE OF CHIVE
- 2 CLOVES OR 1 OLIVE
- A KNIFE

ᗧ When the **wind BLOWS** ᖰ

When the wind blows, everything in nature comes alive. Make a windmill with a simple bottle so you can take part in this celebration!

8 inches (20 cm)

MATERIALS
- 1 PLASTIC BOTTLE
- 1 CORK
- A BIG NAIL
- A STICK AT LEAST 20 INCHES (50 CM) LONG
- A PAIR OF SCISSORS
- ACRYLIC PAINT

1 ☞ Cut off the bottom of the bottle so that the top is about 8 inches (20 cm) long.

☞ *2* Then cut the bottle lengthwise into five equal parts without coming too close to the neck, which must remain solid.

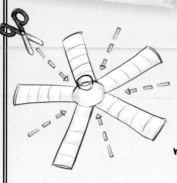

☞ *3* Press down on everything to flatten the parts—except for the neck, of course.

4 ☞ Decorate each arm of the windmill with the paint and then let it dry thoroughly.

☝ *5* While the paint is drying, ask an adult to drive the nail into the stick near one end.

6 ☞
Use the nail to poke a hole in the cork, and then pull the nail back out.

7 ☞
You can either paint your stick or leave it natural.

8 ☞
Put the cut up bottle, neck down, onto the nail.

9 ☞
Stick the cork into the neck and poke it onto the nail.

10 ☞
Everything must be free to spin easily in the wind

Now all you have to do is wait for the next gust of wind so you can admire the movement of your windmill.

BLOW, WIND, BLOW!

A ✍ HOMEMADE 🍃 potpourri

(French for rotten pot!)

What a weird name for such a nice thing with a pleasant smell!

A potpourri is made up of fragrant flower petals, plants, and spices. Before you begin, get a notebook to write down the ingredients of each of your "recipes" and your feelings of the scent it gives off.

some spices (cloves, cardamom seed, a vanilla pod).

Put the bowl in a dry, warm place. Stir the mixture every day to speed up drying.

INTENSIFYING THE FRAGRANCE

For decoration, and to strengthen the scent, add some slices of dried orange or lemon. To make these, cut up the fruits and dry the slices in an oven at low heat. Then add them to the mixture.

FLOWERS

Gather a variety of flowers, especially ones with strong scents (roses, lavender, jasmine), plus a beautiful, bright color.

NATURAL DRYING

Carefully take the petals off and put them into a bowl or a little wicker basket. Add some scented herbs (mint, thyme) and

A strange NAME!

Something rotten that smells good?

In the old days, potpourris were made from fresh ingredients (herbs, spices) that were left to pickle for months until they were *rotten* and had a strong odor.

In the Middle Ages, even the nobles lived in rooms with nothing but a dirt floor. To keep the ground from being so cold, people would cover it with straw and dried herbs, as they did in horse stables.

Every day, this straw, known as litter, was changed. On holidays, flowers were added for a "perfumed" atmosphere.

SMALL DISH OR CLOTH BAG?

Put your potpourri into a little dish so it gives off its scent in the room where it's located. But remember to stir it around occasionally to release the scent.

To make clothing smell nice, store the mixture in a little cloth bag you can put into your closet. In this case, it's a good idea to squeeze the bag occasionally and roll it between your hands to free up the scent of the dried flower and spices.

❧ 𝒜 woven pot ❧

No more messy desk:
Here's how to make a container from recycled materials!
A hands-on project for organizing your pens and pencils!

PREPARE YOUR MATERIALS

Find some large pieces of pretty paper and cut out strips a little over 1 inch (2½ cm) wide and as long as possible. With strips that are 20 inches (50 cm) long, your container will be about 5 inches (12½ cm) tall.

You can use newspaper, wrapping paper, or an old road map. It's up to you to come up with the most interesting types of paper!

❧ HOW TO MAKE IT ❧

1 Cut out sixteen strips of paper.

2 ☞ Fold all the strips lengthwise to make them thicker and stronger.

☞ *3* Put eight folded strips onto the table like this, facing up and down and parallel to one another.

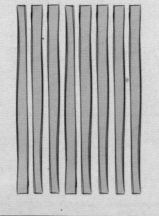

4 ☞

Then do the weaving. Thread in a new strip perpendicular to the first ones by slipping it alternately over and under the vertical strips.

☜ 5

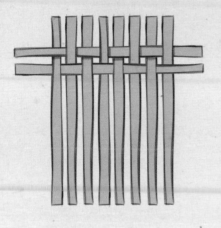

Take a new strip and slide it in the way you did in the last step. But this time, you have to alternate under and over so it's not the same as that strip. If the last strip goes over, this time you go below with the new strip.

6 ☞

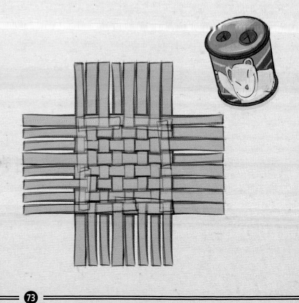

Continue in the same way with the remaining six strips. At the end, your weaving should look like a large cross. To tighten everything, tighten the strips well and put on a couple pieces of tape.

7

Now take two strips of paper in the center of one side. Cross them and start weaving, and add in the other six strips on this same side as you go along.

8

When you weave together all the strips from one side, you create a diamond shape. Hold it in place temporarily at the center, for example, with a clothespin.

9

Weave the other three sides in the same way, always beginning with the two central strips.

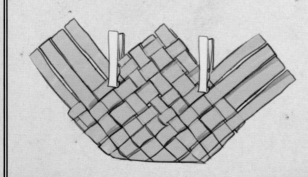

10

Now join all the angles by weaving the sides of the diamond shapes: one side of one diamond to the side of the nearest other diamond, and so forth.

Finish the top of the basket by folding over all the strips toward the inside of the pot. If some pieces of paper are too long, cut them off. Press very hard on the folds at the top to keep them from standing back up.

AND HERE'S THE
FINISHED PRODUCT!
GO GET YOUR
PENS AND PENCILS!

Secret messages

Some secrets are only for your best friend. To keep everyone else from finding out, learn how to use invisible inks and secret codes!

INVISIBLE INKS

LEMON JUICE AND A CANDLE

What's the best invisible ink? Lemon juice!

Dip a fine artist's brush into lemon juice and write your secret on a piece of paper.

It's easy! Once it's dry, the lemon juice becomes invisible. When your friend wants to read your secret, she will have to very carefully move the paper over the flame from a candle (with an adult helping).

When it warms up, the lemon juice becomes brownish and your words appear—as if by magic!

And if you don't have any lemons right at hand, you can write your secret with the eraser you use at school.

In order to read your message, all your friend has to do is scribble all over the paper with the ink from a fountain pen. Then your words will be visible only to her eyes!

SOAP AND BLACK-LEAD PENCIL

There is a much surer way of hiding your secrets. This method uses some items that you surely have around: soap and a pencil with black lead.

Take a small bar of dry soap. With a good pair of scissors carefully cut it to form a rough point.

Use your soap like a large felt-tip marker to write your message. On white paper, write in fairly large capital letters that are easier to decode.

When your friend receives your message, all she has to do is color all over the surface of the paper using broad strokes with a black-lead pencil. The text will appear in white against a black background, because the lead in the pencil leaves no marks on the parts "protected" by the soap.

❧ A CUSTOM SECRET CODE ❧

The simplest secret code involves replacing each letter of the alphabet with a number.

1 = A	10 = J	19 = S
2 = B	11 = K	20 = T
3 = C	12 = L	21 = U
4 = D	13 = M	22 = V
5 = E	14 = N	23 = W
6 = F	15 = O	24 = X
7 = G	16 = P	25 = Y
8 = H	17 = Q	26 = Z
9 = I	18 = R	

SECRET MESSAGE

3-1-12-12 – 13-5 – 17-21-9-3-11!

Solution: Call me quick!

This will help you keep your secrets safe from "enemy" eyes!

TOP SECRET

❧ Games ❧
you can MAKE

If you have forgotten to bring table games on vacation, make some with things you can find where you are staying.

❧ DOMINO PEBBLES ❧

- Find twenty-eight pebbles and clean them carefully.

- Then paint dots on all the stones to reproduce the twenty-eight pieces of a game of dominoes.

☞ **Tip**

To make your game pieces look good and keep the dots and the lines from wearing off, coat them with some clear fingernail polish borrowed from your mom, with her permission.

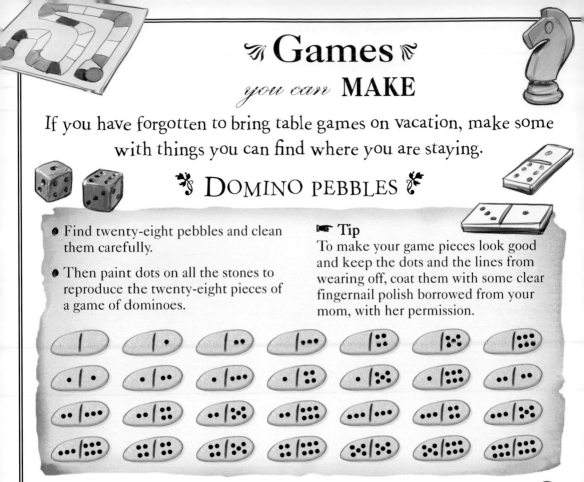

GAME RULES

Turn all the dominoes face down on the table so you can't see the dots.

Mix them up and give six dominoes to each player. The dominoes that are not handed out make up the pot.

Any player who has the double-six must put it down. If no one has the double-six, the double with the greatest number of dots gets to put down first.

Then each player in turn puts a domino at one end of the chain of pieces, provided that the domino put down has

on one of its halves the same number of points as the domino half already in place.

If a player cannot put down a domino, she takes one from the pot.

If this domino can be put down, the player does so. If not, her turn is over.

The first player to put down all her dominoes wins.

MIKADO STICKS

- Find twenty-one little branches of the same size and as straight as possible.
- Ask an adult to remove all the bark from one of the sticks with a knife. This stick will be the mikado.
- Then have four rings of bark removed from five sticks; they will be the samurais.
- Now two rings need to be removed from five other sticks, which will become the mandarins.
- Finally, leave the last ten sticks totally covered in bark. They will be the bonzes.

NAMES FROM ASIA

The sticks in the mikado game have Japanese names. In fact, the old European game of jackstraws was transformed into mikado in China and Japan. Thus, the traditional names for the pieces of different value have been kept.

- The mikado is the emperor of Japan.
- The samurai was a Japanese warrior.
- The mandarin was a powerful Chinese public official.
- The bonze is a Buddhist monk.

RULES OF THE GAME

Hold all the sticks in a bunch in your closed hand. Let them all fall onto the table, boom! Starting with the youngest player, everyone in turn tries to grab one stick. A player may keep a stick if no other stick is moved when she picks it up. She keeps playing as long as she is successful. But watch carefully: as soon as another stick moves, even a tiny bit, her turn is over!

When all the sticks have been picked up, the players add up their points:

- The mikado is worth twenty points.
- Each samurai is worth ten points.
- Each mandarin is worth five points.
- Each bonze is worth three points.

The player with the most points wins!

A Summer Sarong

When you are on vacation, remember to put one of these big scarves into your suitcase. Depending on how you feel, you can wear it as a dress, a skirt, shorts, or harem pants!

A NECKLACE DRESS

1 Hold your sarong horizontally behind you. The center of the big rectangle must be in the middle of your back.

2 Gather the two top corners in front of you and cross them over your chest.

3 Tie a knot behind your neck.

4 You can wear this dress with or without a belt.

❧ AN UNEVEN DRESS ❧

1 👉

Hold the sarong horizontally behind you, but this time position the center of the big rectangle to the side, under one of your arms.

👈 **2**

Pass the front corner under your other arm, toward the rear.

👈 **3**

Place the rear corner in front of your chest.

4 👉

Tie the two corners over one shoulder.

5 👉

This looks really nice when you are coming back from the beach!

❧ A HALTER DRESS ❧

1 This time hold the sarong vertically in front of you.

2 Tie the two top corners behind your neck. Let the rectangle of fabric hang in front of you.

3 Take the two lower corners and pass them between your legs.

4 Pull the fabric up to your waist, bring the two corners in front of you, and tie them in a knot.

Perfect for really hot days!

❧ A SPORTY COMBI-SHORT ❧

1 Hold the sarong vertically in front of you with the top of the rectangle right under your arms. Tie the two top corners behind your back.

2 Let the rectangle hang down in front of you, take the two lower corners, and pass them between your legs.

3 Pull them up to your waist, put the corners together in front of you, and tie a knot.

GREAT FOR A GAME OF
VOLLEYBALL AFTER TAKING A DIP!

UNIQUE HAREM PANTS

1 Hold the sarong vertically in front of you at the level of your waist.

2 Tie the two top corners behind your back.

3 Take the sarong at about its midpoint and pass the fabric between your legs. Bring it up to your waist, and hold it toward the rear.

4 Bring your hands to the front and tie the two corners of the fabric together

5 Now you have nice harem pants that you can wear either short or long, depending on where you take the fabric to tie the second knot.

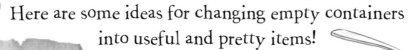

I recycle yogurt CONTAINERS

Here are some ideas for changing empty containers into useful and pretty items!

GARDEN SPIRIT

If you are a gardener at heart, remember that plastic yogurt containers are very useful for making seed beds for flowers and vegetables.

Wash them well and poke some holes in the bottom of the containers so the water can run out.

Fill them halfway with potting soil, put in the seeds, and cover them with a little more soil. Water gently. A few days later, you will see little seedlings that can be replanted in a larger pot.

DECO SPIRIT

🌿 A COLORFUL GARLAND 🌿

MATERIALS
- SOME SMALL YOGURT CONTAINERS (THE TYPE WITH FRUIT FLAVORING)
- A PAIR OF SCISSORS
- A BLACK FELT-TIP PEN
- A HOBBY KNIFE
- A LIGHT STRING

1 Start by thoroughly washing the yogurt containers. Cut the tops off the containers (the square parts). Use the felt-tip pen to draw the shape you want to give the petals of your container: rounded, pointed, etc.

2 Cut the shapes out around the lines.

3 Ask an adult to make a slit in the bottom of each container using the hobby knife, and to insert a bulb from the light string.

4 Remember to alternate containers of different colors; this will be much more cheerful!

DECORATIVE GLASS LAMPS

Glass jars are a great starting point for decorating a table!

Start by washing and drying the containers thoroughly.

If you are in a hurry, you can just slip a little tea light onto the bottom. This is a quick but effective lamp!

If you want a fancier lamp, fill the containers halfway with water.

Float little tea candles on the water. Move the containers to the table slowly, otherwise the flames might go out.

And why not use sand instead of water? Prop up the candle in the sand, and in order to make everything prettier, wrap the container in some colored string.

You can also put on a piece of fabric and hold it in place with the colored string or another ribbon.

If you invite your friends to dinner, the string can be used to hold a little piece of paper with the name of each of your friends. At a formal dinner, this works well for showing where the people are supposed to sit!

☞ Other styles

You can slip in some other items under the colored string to give your lamp a more personal touch— for example, a cinnamon stick, a cut flower, or a rose petal.

Always keep some yogurt containers handy—there is always something you can do with them!

Seasonal DRINKS

Four recipes to keep you stocked up on vitamins all year long!

❧ LEMONADE: A SUMMER THIRST QUENCHER ❧

INGREDIENTS

- 4 LEMONS
- 1 CUP (200 G) OF SUGAR
- 1 QUART (1 L) OF WATER
- A LARGE HEAT-RESISTANT CONTAINER

- Carefully grate the peels of four lemons.
- Put the gratings into the container and sprinkle with sugar.
- Let sit for a half hour.
- With an adult's help, boil the water and pour it over the mixture. Let everything cool down.
- Squeeze the juice out of the lemons and pour it into the mixture.
- Put the bowl into the refrigerator. This lemonade is served nice and cold!

☞ **Tip:**
Add some ice cubes and lemon slices for decoration.

If you want sparkling lemonade, you can add club soda to the mixture!

❧ CITRUS JUICE FOR KEEPING UP YOUR ENERGY IN THE WINTER ❧

- Take one lemon and squeeze out the juice.
- Beat the egg yolks in a bowl.
- Add the milk, the citrus juice, and the sugar.
- Put the mixture into the refrigerator. Before serving, add the juice from the last lemon.

☞ **Tip:**

For a more zesty juice, add a grapefruit to the recipe and leave out one or two spoonfuls of sugar. You can also substitute brown sugar for the white sugar and taste the difference!

INGREDIENTS

- 5 ORANGES AND 3 LEMONS
- 8 TABLESPOONS OF SUGAR
- 3 CUPS (¾ L) OF MILK
- 4 EGG YOLKS

SPRING VEGETABLE JUICE

Did you notice? This is a vegetable juice—with fruits!

- Wash the vegetables well and peel them.

- Cut them into small pieces and run them through the blender or juicer.

- Pour the mixture into a pitcher and add the lemon juice that you squeezed.

- Put the mixture into the refrigerator and serve it cold.

☞ **Tip:**

Substitute a beet for the lemon juice and mix it in with the other fruits and vegetables, and it will give your juice some color!

INGREDIENTS
- 4 APPLES
- 6 CARROTS
- 4 STALKS OF CELERY
- 1 LEMON

FROSTING THE GLASS

To give a cocktail touch to your glasses, you can frost them. To do that, squeeze one lemon and pour the juice into a dish. Fill another dish with granulated sugar. Dip the rim of the glasses first into the juice and then into the sugar, and immediately put them into the refrigerator. A frozen-sugary sensation is guaranteed!

TOMATO JUICE FOR FEELING PERKY IN THE FALL

INGREDIENTS
- 6 RIPE TOMATOES
- 2 STALKS OF CELERY
- 2 LEMONS

- With an adult's help, boil some water in a pan.

- Slide the tomatoes into the water for a few seconds and then run them under cold water. Now it's easy to peel them.

- Cut the celery into little pieces and run the pieces through the mixer with the tomatoes.

- If you don't like tomato seeds, you can strain the mixture through a sieve.

- Now add the lemon juice and put the mixture into the refrigerator.

 Tip:

For a thicker mixture, substitute two avocados for the celery.

A Crazy GAME: Monkey QUARTER

A fast game that requires no materials and is tons of fun!

The players sit on the floor in a circle—everyone's mission is to avoid turning into a monkey, and that's not so easy to do!

STARTING THE GAME

The youngest person starts by calling out a letter—for example, she says D. That means that she is thinking of a word that contains this letter.

The following player must choose between two possible actions:

- **Action number one:** Call out another letter, such as E, which means that she knows a word that contains the two letters D and E (*dent* or *reduce*, for example).

- **Action number two:** challenge the last player to say her word.

COMPLICATIONS

Of course, it's easy with two letters! But watch out, the game continues—and each player in turn adds one letter. It will become more difficult to find a word!

BLUFFING

If the letters called out after D and E are F, U, T, and Y, you surely have no idea what word to throw out. So challenge the last player; she is required to say the word she is thinking. Or else you can add a new letter at random, pretending to be very confident—so that the following player thinks that you really have a word in mind. That is what's called the bluff!

CHALLENGING

The player challenged must immediately say the word that has all the letters involved. If she succeeds, her challenger gets a monkey quarter.

If the player challenged cannot say a word, she's the one who gets the monkey quarter.

THE FIRST MONKEY QUARTER

A monkey quarter is a sort of penalty. As soon as a player gets a first monkey quarter, she must raise one hand, and she can't put it down until the end of the game.

THE OTHER THREE QUARTERS

If the player gets a second monkey quarter, she must raise her other hand and keep it raised until the end of the game.

With the third monkey quarter, the player may put her two hands on her head.

With the fourth monkey quarter, the player becomes a complete monkey. She can lower her arms, but the other players continue playing without speaking to her.

So, in the course of the game, the players have different quarters. One might have her first, while another has her fourth.

THE REMEDY

The player who has turned into a monkey can become a human again. To do that, she has to force one of the other players to speak to her. Any trick is permitted to achieve this—suggesting a drink, telling a joke, saying a letter or a word as if she were still part of the game. All it takes is for one player to respond to the monkey, and, bingo, the monkey is "cured" and comes back into the game. Then the player who talked too much gets a monkey quarter!

GUARANTEED FUN!

A Real Magician

Here are some easy tricks you can learn that always amaze people.

★ THE THREE ALWAYS WINS ★

PREPARE THE TRICK

When nobody can see you, take a deck of cards and remove the four threes (the three of hearts, the three of diamonds, the three of spades, and the three of clubs). Put these cards on the top of the deck.

THE SHOW BEGINS

In front of your audience, split the deck into three stacks that you put on the table face down like this:

★ Put the first four cards onto the first stack without showing them (you are the only one who knows that these four cards are threes).

★ Put the next three cards onto the second stack (you don't know what these cards are, but that doesn't matter; the only thing that counts is that there are only three cards).

★ Put all the remaining cards onto the third stack.

Tell the audience that you can guess which of these three stacks a person is going to choose. Add that you are so sure of yourself that you are going to write the answer *here*, on this little piece of paper.

Then take a pencil and a piece of paper and write on it the number 3, in private, so no one can see.

Fold the paper and put it on the table near the stacks of cards.

Then explain that these three stacks of cards are called from left to right 1 (the four threes), 2 (the three cards), and 3 (the rest of the deck).

YOU WIN!

Ask a person to choose one of the stacks, and then to turn over the cards from the chosen stack.

★ If it's the first pile that gets turned over (the one with the four *threes*), you say, *I knew it!* And you unfold your little piece of paper with the number 3 written on it. *Applause.*

★ If the second stack is chosen (the one with three cards), you say, *I knew it!* And you unfold your paper, and then you show that this deck contains precisely *three cards*. *Applause.*

★ If it's the third stack (the one in the third position), you say, *I knew it!* You unfold the paper and point out that it really is the *third stack*. *Applause.*

★ THE RAINBOW ★

PREPARE THE TRICK

Find a packet of colored felt-tip markers and make sure that none of them is dried out.

THE SHOW BEGINS

Put the packet onto the table in front of you and tell audience that you have a telepathic gift when it comes to felt-tip markers!

Ask a volunteer to take the packet of felt-tip markers and step behind you. Have the person choose a marker and show it to the audience without your seeing it, and then put the marker into your hands, which are folded behind your back.

THERE'S A TRICK?

While the volunteer is returning to the audience, quickly remove the cap from

the marker and make a small dot on one of your fingers. Put the cap back on the marker. Of course, your hands are still folded behind your back. While making grand, mysterious gestures, move the marked hand in front of your eyes.

YOU WIN!

Then, after pretending to search a little, say the color!

Applause!

PREPARE THE TRICK

Take a small coin—say, a nickel or a dime.

THE SHOW BEGINS

Tell the audience that you are able to command t████n. In fact, you are going to order it to go into your arm! Attention, everyone, are you ready to witness this great session of magic? Some people may wish to close their eyes!

Bend your arm up to your chest and show the coin that you are holding in your other hand.

Now rub this coin on your bent arm while you say some magic phrases. Because the coin is small, people can't see it when you rub it on your bent arm.

But oops! How clumsy you are! You drop the coin onto the floor! Let the audience have a laugh at your (pretend) clumsiness and continue the trick as if nothing had happened. But, look, when you open your hand that was holding the coin, there's nothing there! The coin really has disappeared, surely by going into your arm!

THERE'S A TRICK!

In reality, you dropped the coin on purpose. While it is on the floor, take advantage of the opportunity to pass it from one hand to the other! The audience believes that the coin is still in your hand that is rubbing your arm, but now it's in the hand of your bent arm. Magic!

YOU WIN!

Ask a person from the audience to come up very close to you. Hold out your bent arm and put your hand with the coin up close to the person's ear. Ah! What is this person hiding in his/her ear? Then take the coin out of your hand as if it came from his/her ear.

Applause.

PREPARE THE TRICK

For this trick you need a paper clip and a piece of tape.

Put the paper clip the long way onto your thumbnail. Cut a tiny piece of tape and stick it onto the end of your nail to hold the paper clip in place.

Bend your thumb and put the index finger of the same hand over your thumbnail. Your index finger thus hides the piece of tape. Now hold your fingers still.

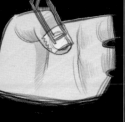

THE SHOW BEGINS

Tell the audience that your magic powers allow you to make small objects disappear, such as this paper clip.

Ask a person to come up to within a step of you, say any magic words she wants, and then blow on the paper clip. At the instant when the person blows, open your hand all at once! Bingo! The paper clip has disappeared!

THERE'S A TRICK!

Of course, the paper clip didn't fly away! Because, now you show only the palm of your hand, there is no way to know that the paper clip is still stuck to your thumbnail, but it is well hidden!

More applause!

Bravo! What a magician!

Identifying wild FLOWERS

White, yellow, red, blue—they blossom in the wild! Learn to identify them.

JUST WHAT ARE FLOWERS?

Flowers are the organs that assure the reproduction of the plant. Flowers bear the male organs, the stamens, and the female organs, the pistils. In gathering pollen from the flowers, insects transport stamens to the pistils of other flowers, which are fertilized in turn, giving rise to new plants.

DAISY

The daisy, with its bright yellow center and its tight rows of white and slightly pink petals, is an easy flower to recognize. It blossoms throughout much of the year and likes the sun, because it opens around noon and follows the sun until sundown.

OXEYE DAISY

A cousin of the daisy, the oxeye daisy is larger and blossoms between May and July. People often play "she loves me, she loves me not" with its petals.

PRIMROSE

The primrose likes moist ground. It announces the spring in March or April!

DANDELION

The dandelion flower is bright yellow, with lots of petals on a strong stalk. You can find the dandelion from March to November. It turns into a feather duster. When you blow on it, you send out dandelion seeds, and they may give rise to other flowers far away.

POPPY

Poppies—you can't miss these flowers! With their red color, hairy stalks, and wrinkled-looking petals, they are a standout in fields and along roadsides. They blossom from May to July.

LILY OF THE VALLEY

The lily of the valley blossoms from April through June. In the wild, it grows in the woods. You can recognize it by its little white flowers (with a nice smell) and its broad, thick leaves.

BLUEBELLS

The bluebell is recognizable by its blue petals shaped like little bells. The leaves are long and slender. It is found in the underbrush from April through June.

JONQUIL

The flower called *jonquil* is, in fact, a yellow narcissus. It is recognizable by its long, yellow bell surrounded by petals that seem to be sticking out a bit! It blossoms from April to June in fields and forests.

RESPECTING PROTECTED FLOWERS

It's fun to gather flowers to make bouquets and potpourris—that will fill the house with fragrance, but be careful. Some species are endangered.

Before you take off on a hike, find out what protected species live in your area so you can recognize them. Here are some that you can admire and photograph, but shouldn't pick.

The **purple violet** with its little hooks grows in high mountain meadows.

This variety of **angelica** lives in mild to subarctic regions of North America.

This little **iris** used to be very widespread, but now it is in danger of disappearing.

Celebrating MUSIC

Feel like playing some music? Here's how to make some instruments for a concert with your friends.

DRUMSTICKS

Every band has percussion instruments, but you need sticks to beat a drum!

MATERIALS
- SOME CORKS
- SOME LIQUID GLUE
- SOME WOOD STICKS (BAMBOO, PENCIL)
- SOME YARN (OR COTTON TWINE)

1 Ask an adult to make a hole in as many corks as you will need to make your sticks. Each hole must be the same diameter as each piece of wood.

2 Put a little glue into the bottom of each hole.

3 Poke the sticks into the corks.

4 Coil the yarn around the corks until the entire length is wrapped.

5 Hold everything in place with a drop of glue.

6 You can make all kinds of sticks by wrapping the cork with different materials: string, wire, or rubber bands. Every material makes a different sound.

MATERIALS

- CLAY POTS OF DIFFERENT SIZES
- 1 NUT
- 1 STRING ABOUT 12 INCHES
  (30 CM) LONG
- ACRYLIC PAINT
- A PAINTBRUSH

🎵 UNIQUE BELLS 🎵

Now that your sticks are ready, make some bells you can strike.

1 👉 Decorate the pots any way you choose with the paint. This won't change the sound of the bells, but they will be prettier to look at!

👈 *3* Thread the string through the hole on the bottom of the pot and let the nut hang inside. Make a big knot on the outside of the pot. If the hole is too big, roll the rest of the string around the pot and make a knot. Now your bell is done! Use one of your homemade sticks for striking the pot. Bing! Bong! What a rhythm!

👈 *2*

Tie a nut to the end of the string with a good tight knot.

VARIATION

Make several bells with pots of different sizes in order to vary the sounds.

Get a board. Ask an adult to drill a few little holes. Tie the pots to the board with the string that sticks out of the bottom. Place the pots from the smallest to the largest.

Rest the ends of the board on chairs and use the instrument like a xylophone.

NIFTY GUITARS

You really need a stringed instrument to accompany the music of the bells! How about making a guitar? It's very easy.

☞ **1** Find some metal or wood containers: pots, big salad bowls, strong boxes—anything that is solid and empty.

2 ☞

Wrap each "guitar body" with large, tight rubber bands arranged side by side For best results, use rubber bands of different thicknesses.

☞ **3**

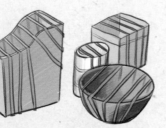

To play, pluck the rubber bands! Twang! Twang!

THE WHISTLING COMB

Do you need some melody in addition to the rhythms produced by your bells and the notes from the rubber bands? Then add a little whistling comb to your band!

☞ **1** All you need is a comb and a piece of wax paper a little longer than the comb. Put the comb on the piece of paper.

2
Fold the four sides over the comb.

3 ☞
Crease well.

4 ☞
Place the comb protected by the wax paper so that it touches your lips and blow out softly. Zzzzz. This makes a strange sound.

Are all the instruments of your neat orchestra ready? On with the music!

A FAIRY Headpiece

A crown of flowers for a little wood nymph!

If you go to a costume party or you simply want to be the most beautiful girl on a summer night, here's how to make a floral headband worthy of the greatest princess.

1 You need about twenty of your favorite flowers. When you cut them, be sure to leave a stem about 2 inches (5 cm) long. If you make your crown from fresh flowers, it will last for only one evening before it wilts. But with little fake flowers, you can wear your fairy crown several times. You can find these flowers at a flower shop, a decoration store, or a hobby shop.

2 Attach the first flower to the cord with adhesive ribbon. To do this, lay the stem along the cord and wrap the piece of adhesive around it once or twice.

3 Put on the flowers one after the other and attach them all in the same way.

4 Tie the ribbon to one end of the cord; make sure to leave at least 6 inches (15 cm) free at the end.

5 Wrap the ribbon around the cord to hide the adhesive ribbon. Careful: Don't pass it over the flowers; go between them!

Once you reach the other end of the cord, tie one more tight knot. **6**

To wear your crown of flowers, all you have to do is tie the two ends of the ribbon behind your head, under your hair, to keep it firmly in place. Let the two pieces of ribbon hang down your back.

There you have it: a beautiful loop!

★ Hedgehog SUPERSTARS ★

Do you love these cute little animals?
Here's how to celebrate them.

The hedgehog is a very useful little animal because it eats all kinds of small creatures that harm gardens (slugs, snails, insects, and even little snakes), before eating some berries for dessert. Now it can be part of your table decorations.

🌿 PINECONE HEDGEHOGS 🌿

👉 Glue some white beads onto a pinecone to make the eyes, and some hazelnut shells for the ears.

It's easy! Now all you have to do is decorate your table with a family of little hedgehogs with bodies made from pinecones.

🚩 VARIANT
For a spinier hedgehog, stick some pine needles between the scales of the pinecone. Poke! Poke!

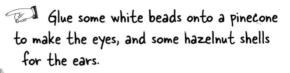

✤ A HEDGEHOG CARDHOLDER ✤

MATERIALS
- AN OLD PAPERBACK BOOK
- 1 SHEET OF WHITE PAPER
- 1 SHEET OF BLACK PAPER
- 1 LEAD PENCIL
- 1 PAIR OF SCISSORS
- LIQUID GLUE

1 Open the book. Fold over the bottom of the first page by folding the bottom corner to the central fold of the book.

2 Now fold the left side of this first page to line it up with the central fold of the book. Crease the fold.

3 Using the pencil, trace the shape of the fold on the cover of the book. Cut along this line. Fold all the pages in the same way.

4 Cut out two little circles from the white paper, and then two smaller circles from the black paper. Glue a black circle onto each white circle. You have just made the hedgehog's eyes! Glue them to the slanted part of your folded book.

5 You can also glue on two small ears or a cute little nose in the same way.

6 Now slide some photos or nice drawings between the pages of the book to display them!

HEDGEHOG CAKE FOR DESSERT

And to finish up the meal, serve a tasty hedgehog cake!

☞ PREPARE A FROSTED POUND CAKE AS FOLLOWS:

INGREDIENTS FOR THE CAKE

- 4 OUNCES (120 G) OF BUTTER (1 STICK)
- ½ CUP (120 G) OF SUGAR
- ½ CUP (120 G) OF FLOUR
- 2 LARGE EGGS (OR 3 SMALL ONES)
- 1 TEASPOON OF BAKING POWDER

1 Melt the butter for a few seconds in the microwave. Mix in the flour and the baking powder. Now stir all the ingredients together.

2 With an adult's help, preheat the oven to 350°F (175°C). Butter a cake pan, pour in the dough, and put the pan into the oven, being very careful not to burn yourself.

3 After forty minutes, you can take out your cake and let it cool. When it has cooled down, cut off two angles from the same side for making the head of your hedgehog.

Maybe if you put these two pieces of cake out in your yard, they will bring out some hedgehog friends.

PREPARE THE FROSTING

1 In a pan, melt the chocolate with the liquid cream. Put the gelatin into some cold water for as long as it takes to do the following.

2 In another pan, mix the thick cream and the sugar, and then bring it to a boil.

3 Then add in the gelatin and the contents of the first pan. Mix well. Pour your frosting over your hedgehog cake. Coat it all over!

FINISH YOUR HEDGEHOG CAKE

Decorate your hedgehog by sticking in the finger rolls to represent the animal's spines. For the ears, stick in the ladyfinger cookies. Use candies or dried or candied fruits for the eyes and the nose.

Yum! No mercy for the hedgehog cake!

❧ A flower for DECORATION ❧

Make a totally original cloth flower using odds
and ends salvaged from here and there.

1 ☞ Cut a big circle about 2½ inches (6 cm) in diameter out of the cardboard.

2½ inches

☞ *2* Find some small pieces of fabric in colors that go well together: ribbons, a piece of scarf, a pretty lace, a dishcloth, some packing twine. Cut all these found objects into strips 6 inches (15 cm) long. Fold each strip in half and glue the two ends together on the cardboard. This will form the petals of your flower.

3 ☞ From the cardboard, cut out another circle smaller than the first one. When you have finished forming the petals with the pieces of fabric, glue the smaller cardboard circle in the center to close up and strengthen the flower.

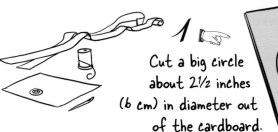

4 ☞ Put the button in the center. Make a knot at the end of the thread and sew through the flower by passing the needle through one of the holes. Pull the thread tight. On the underside, poke through in another place, go through the center, and then through another hole.

☞ *5* Continue until you think the flower is strong enough. Tie a knot and cut the thread off. There's your cloth flower that can be used as a brooch, a barrette, or a necklace.

☛ BROOCH

1 On the back of the brooch, glue a safety pin with glue.

2 In winter, don't hide your pretty brooch: Pin it to your coat. You can also pin it to items such as your school bag or a scarf.

☛ BARRETTE

1 Glue the flower on a barrette instead of a safety pin and you will have a very pretty hair clip!

2 Because the flower is large, gather your ponytail a little lower than usual so that your flower doesn't get bent.

☛ HEADBAND

You can use thread to attach your flower to a headband.

☛ NECKLACE

Put a long ribbon or a pretty lace trim through the loop of one petal to make a really cool pendant!

You decide what your flower will be used to decorate!

⫷ BEACH Comets ⫸

Had enough lounging around the beach? Feel like getting some fun exercise with your friends? Check out these beach comets!

MATERIALS
- PLASTIC BAGS OF DIFFERENT COLORS
- SOME RICE OR SAND
- 2 RUBBER BANDS
- 2 STRINGS, INCLUDING ONE AT LEAST 20 INCHES (50 CM) LONG
- A PAIR OF SCISSORS

1 ☞ Cut a square at least 6 inches (15 cm) on a side from a plastic bag.

2 ☞ Put three handfuls of sand or rice into a little pile in the center of your square.

3 ☜ Close the pile of sand inside the plastic square. Use the shorter string to close it up with a good tight knot.

4 ☞ Now cut some long strips about 3/4 inch (1½ cm) wide from the plastic bags or from thin, light paper, such as crepe paper. Put the strips together in a bundle.

5 ☜ Hold all these strips together tightly at one end with a rubber band. This is the tail of the comet.

6

Now all you have to do is attach this tail to the little bag of rice or sand using another rubber band.

7

At the same spot, tie on a string about 12 to 16 inches (30 to 40 cm) long and let it hang down.

A NEW BEACH SPORT: THROWING COMETS!

☛ When each of your friends has made a comet, line them up side by side. Leave at least 6 feet (2 m) between people so you don't hurt each other or get the tails of your comets tangled up. Grab the end of the string in one hand and let the comet and its colorful tail hang down.

☛ At an agreed signal, spin the comets over your heads like a cowboy with a lasso.

☛ Count to five. On five, let fly!

The comets take off. The one who sends hers the farthest from the starting line is crowned the Queen of the Comets!

Party PROJECTS

All you need to decorate a corner of the table and turn a simple meal into a party is a little bit of colored paper! Invite your guests to dinner at a festive, cheerful table in your home!

MATERIALS
- DIFFERENT KINDS OF PAPER
- GLUE
- A PAIR OF SCISSORS

A GARLAND

1 Find two kinds of paper in contrasting colors, such as gift wrap, crepe paper, or even aluminum foil used in the kitchen. Cut a long strip about 1½ inches (4 cm) wide from each paper.

2 Put the end of the first strip flat on the table. Put the end of the second strip on top and perpendicular to the first one.

3 Glue or staple the two strips of paper together.

4 Fold the first strip of paper over the second.

5 Then fold the second over the first, and again and again, until there is no more paper.

6 Glue together the last two squares of paper that you folded.

7

Grab the two ends of your garland, move your hands apart, and there you have it!

8 👉

Make several garlands of different lengths; then look around and decide where to hang them: on a curtain rod, over a picture, around the base of a lamp.

🌿 LACE PLACEMATS 🌿

1 👉

Put the pieces of paper on top of one another, then fold the whole bundle in half, and then in half again (and once more if possible).

MATERIALS
- LARGE PIECES OF MULTICOLORED PAPER
- A PAIR OF SCISSORS
- GLUE

2 👉

Draw some geometric designs spaced out an inch or so (a few centimeters) apart all around the top sheet.

Unfold the placemats and enjoy the results!

3 👉

Cut out the thicknesses all at once along your designs.

DECORATING GLASSES

To complete the series of placemats.

☞ **1**
Take one of your placemats and cut it into several strips about 1½ inches (4 cm) wide.

☞ **2**
Wrap one of the strips around the middle of a glass.

3 ☞
After one turn, glue the strip to hold it in place and cut off the extra paper.

Now your glasses are decorated to match the placemats!

GIFT BASKET

Two-color garlands and placemats have brightened up the décor, but for the party to be complete, offer a little gift to each guest at the end of the meal. And for each gift, you can prepare a pretty paper basket that's much more original than the usual wrapping!

MATERIALS
- SHEETS OF 8½ × 11 INCHES (A4) PAPER
- A DRAWING COMPASS
- A PAIR OF SCISSORS

1 ☞
Take a piece of paper and fold it in half.

2 Round the two upper corners with the scissors.

3 Then cut out the handle for the basket—a shape big enough for your fingers to reach into.

4 Using the compass, draw some semicircles spaced about 1 inch (2½ cm) apart. There should be an even number of semicircles, and they should be parallel to one another.

5 Cut out some sections of the semicircles using the scissors.

6 When you place the mini-gift inside the basket, its weight will stretch out the slits cut in the paper. You have made a real little basket that your guests are sure to love!

Now all you have to do is find a nice little present to make.

A Scent of TIMES PAST

Here's a trick to make your clothes smell good and give your closet a nice perfumed scent. Make this spindle of lavender the way our great-grandmothers did.

Lavender blooms during the summer, in July. Cut about twenty stalks and make them as long as possible.

1 ☞

MATERIALS
- A PAIR OF SCISSORS
- SOME TWINE
- A LONG, FAIRLY NARROW RIBBON

3 Form an even bouquet with all the flowers at the same height; it doesn't matter if the stems are different lengths.

☞ **2** Remove all the little leaves and keep only the bare stems and the flowers on the ends.

☞ **4** Tie the twine tight just below the flowers.

Note!
In order to make this spindle, the stems of the flowers must be very flexible. So you have to make it immediately after cutting the lavender. Otherwise, put your bouquet into a vase with some water to make the stems more flexible until you can deal with them.

5 👉 Pinch the end of the pretty ribbon under the twine and let it hang down along the stalks.

6 👉 Fold down each stem and the ribbon at the level of the twine that you tied before, to form a sort of umbrella so that all the stalks surround the flowers.

👈 **7** Start weaving the ribbon among the stems by going over two stems, then under one. Again, go over two stems and then under one, and so forth, in a spiral—until all the flowers are hidden by the ribbon and the folded stems.

👈 **8** Now all you have to do is to tie a tight, pretty knot under the flowers.

9 👉 Cut all the stems off to the same length so your spindle looks nice.

Hang your lavender spindle in your closet by the ribbon and

enjoy the wonderful scent every time you open the door!

Your JEWELRY Bowl

To keep from losing track of your jewelry, put it all into a pretty bowl that you make yourself!

1 ☞

In the kitchen, choose a container with a shape that you like. Find some thick, pretty paper or some sheets of drawing paper in different colors. Cut out strips about ¾ inch (2 cm) wide.

☞ 2

You can use all types of paper for making this bowl. The paper must not be shiny; otherwise, the coating on it will keep the glue from penetrating. Put a good coat of oil on the whole inside of the bowl.

3 ☞

Arrange a first layer of strips into the bowl; then glue a second layer on top of them. Put in each new strip so it partly overlaps the last one. In all, put two or three layers of paper into the bowl.

☞ 4

Let it dry. Then carefully remove the bowl that served as a model for the paper bowl that you have just made.

5 Continue to be very careful so you don't crush your paper bowl; put it in a spot where it can dry. If you are really in a rush, you can gain some time by using a hair dryer.

6 Now cut out some other strips from paper of another color, or simply from newspaper. Once the mold is nice and dry, carefully glue the little strips of paper onto the outside one by one. You will have to put on at least two layers of paper to make your bowl strong.

7 To decorate your jewelry bowl, as soon as it is good and dry, you can make some little holes all around the bowl with a paper punch. Slide a couple of strands of yarn through each hole; make a knot in the end to form a sort of pom-pom.

No more lost jewelry!

A DREAM Catcher

Keep bad dreams away the way the Native Americans do: Make a thoughtful gift and an ornament "world-deco" style!

Papooses were the children of Native Americans. Every night, their mothers told them fabulous stories so they would fall asleep. But the mothers had a little trick, a secret: dream catchers that they made and hung above their sleeping children so the children could enjoy a peaceful, pleasant sleep.

MATERIALS

- 4 WOOD BRANCHES
- SOME STRING
- SOME NARROW RIBBON OR STRING
- WIRE
- GLUE
- SHEARS
- VARIOUS LITTLE DECORATIONS (FEATHERS, SHELLS, DRIED FLOWERS)

1 ☞

Ask an adult to cut four branches of the same length with the shears. Using the pieces of string (or the ribbon or colored wire, depending on the style you choose for your dream catcher), tie the branches together to make a square.

☜ *2*

Bend the wire into a circle. Note: This circle must fit perfectly inside the square formed by the branches.

3 👉

Now take the ribbon, or if you want to give your dream catcher a more rustic appearance, the string, which looks more natural. If you want a livelier design, choose some yarn the color of your dreams. Tie the end of the ribbon or the string to the wire circle.

👈 **4** Go across the circle several times to form a large star with your string: Each point of the star is tied to the circle by making two or three turns around the wire.

5 👉

Now all you have to do is decorate this star by gluing or tying on all kinds of items: little shells, dried seaweed, and little pieces of driftwood—if you want to dream about being at the seashore;

6 👉

Acorns, hazelnuts, little pebbles and dried flowers—to make you think of a vacation in the country;

7

Beads, mini–jewels, or little toys you find in your room—to dream about the time when you were a baby;

8

Feathers and little colored papers, folded items on which you write some nice words—for a really sweet night.

9 Now attach the circle to the wood square with four pieces of string, one on each side of the square. You can also decorate the wood frame by attaching other pretty items to it or by hanging some short strings from the bottom and stringing some beads onto them. Tie a long string in the center of the top branch and attach your dream catcher to the wall or the ceiling, like a mobile.

10

Here's your finished dream catcher! Every night, look at it before you go to sleep. Think of the papooses whose mothers told them that the worst nightmares would never make it through this trap and would be imprisoned in the weave of the string!

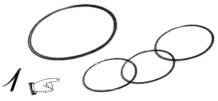

1 ☞

Do step 2 on page 118. Repeat this step three times but with shorter lengths of wire. That way you will end up with three new circles that are much smaller than the first one.

☞ *3* Tie one end of one of the ribbons to the center, at the bottom of the big circle. Tie another piece on each side of this same circle.

☞ *2* Cut five pieces of ribbon the same length as half the height of the big circle.

☞ *4* Now attach one of the little circles to each of these ribbons.

☞ *5* Attach a feather (or anything else you want) to the end of the two ribbons left over.

6 ☞

Then attach these two charms: one to the circle on the right, and the other to the one on the left.

☞ *7*

Do steps 3 to 5 on page 119. Cut a piece of ribbon longer than the previous ones. Tie it to the decoration of your choice. For a prettier version, choose an item that's larger than the other ones and attach the whole thing to the little circle in the middle. You have now made a different form of dream catcher that's just as good as the other ones!

My Sketches

My Notes

My Sketches

My Notes

Publication Director: Isabelle Jeuge-Maynart
Editorial Director: Séverine Charbonnel-Bojman
Editor: Geraldine Tranchant
Art Director: Laurent Carré
Illustrations: Jocelyn Millet
Cover Design: Miyo Edit (Christophe Petit and Gaëlle Moniment)
Proofreader: Chantal Pagès, Pierre Vallas, and Henri Goldszal
Production: Martine Toudert

All photos in this book are © copyright Thinkstock.

All inquiries should be addressed to:
Barron's Educational Series, Inc.
250 Wireless Boulevard
Hauppauge, NY 11788
www.barronseduc.com

ISBN: 978-0-7641-6610-5

Library of Congress Catalog Number: 2012944150
Date of Manufacture: February 2015
Manufactured by: Heshan Astros Printing Ltd., Guangdong, China

Product conforms to all applicable CPSC and CPSIA 2008 standards.
No lead or phthalate hazard.

Printed in China
9 8 7 6